Praise for
Jesus Was an Airborne Ranger

"John McDougall 'gets it.' This combat-hardened warrior shatters misconceptions about Jesus, the Ultimate Warrior. Yes, Jesus is gentle, meek, and mild, but he's also tougher than the metal spikes that fastened him to the cross for our sins and more powerful than the powers of hell that could not keep him in the grave. John rightly portrays Jesus as the Ranger we want to follow and the God we bow to worship. Read this book!"

—CHAPLAIN (COLONEL) SCOTT MCCHRYSTAL, U.S. Army, Ret.

"Finally! A book that accurately depicts King Jesus as the tough man the Bible describes. I'm convinced great men must have a great leader to follow. Unfortunately, many pastors, chaplains, and theologians paint the picture of Jesus being weak and timid. *Jesus Was an Airborne Ranger* is for anyone who wants to know how this one man, who lived thousands of years ago, is still changing the world today."

—CHAPLAIN (MAJOR) JEFF STRUECKER, U.S. Army

"I've served with some of the nation's most elite units: Green Berets, Navy SEALs, and Delta Operators. The best of the best. But I've never met a warrior who can match Jesus of Nazareth. In this book, Chaplain McDougall has taken the ancient scripture 'The Lord is a warrior' and brought it to life in a modern Special Operations context. *Jesus Was an Airborne Ranger* will forever change the way you think about our Savior!"

—LIEUTENANT GENERAL WILLIAM "JERRY" BOYKIN, Executive Vice President, Family Research Council

"Chaplain John McDougall caught my eye with his unexpected title and then brilliantly made his case as I turned each page. This book is biblically solid, carefully crafted, and lasered to speak to the hearts and minds of men who follow the Lord Jesus Christ. I think pastors and men's leaders will buy this book by the case for their men."

—STEVE FARRAR, author of *Point Man*

"A gripping account of the salvation history of Jesus Christ as seen through the eyes of a professional soldier and military chaplain. Written from the heart and soul of a U.S. Army Airborne Ranger, Chaplain John McDougall challenges the reader to view Jesus in his image as *Christus Victor*—the 'victorious Christ' who conquered sin, evil, death, and the grave. This compelling book is a must read for those servant leaders who choose Jesus to 'lead the way' in this life and into eternity."

—CHAPLAIN (MAJOR GENERAL) DOUG CARVER, U.S. Army, Ret.

"Chaplain McDougall brings his 'been there, done that' experience to this project, sharing insights that will animate and motivate men—especially military men—to follow the warrior Christ. So many men see Christianity as a threat to their perception of manhood, while nothing could be further from the truth. This book will make men want to get into the fight for something much bigger than themselves."

—CHUCK HOLTON, former Ranger, author of *Making Men: Five Steps to Growing Up*

"Don't let the sandals fool you—the Jesus of Scripture unveiled by John McDougall was a leader of uncommon bravery, fiercely devoted to accomplishing his divine mission. His example serves as a challenge to us all. Our purpose and salvation is not to be found in comfort, but rather in hardship, struggle, and sacrifice."

—CRAIG MULLANEY, author of *The Unforgiving Minute: A Soldier's Education*

"What a powerful story of a Savior who set the example for us to follow—to lay down His life to ransom the world. John McDougall is the ideal guide in exploring the world's greatest rescue mission; I invite you to join him!"

—CAPTAIN NATE SELF, Army Ranger and author of *Two Wars*

JESUS WAS AN AIRBORNE RANGER

JESUS WAS AN AIRBORNE RANGER

Find Your Purpose Following the Warrior Christ

JOHN MCDOUGALL
CHAPLAIN, U.S. ARMY RANGERS

MULTNOMAH
BOOKS

JESUS WAS AN AIRBORNE RANGER
PUBLISHED BY MULTNOMAH BOOKS
12265 Oracle Boulevard, Suite 200
Colorado Springs, Colorado 80921

Scripture quotations are taken from the Holy Bible, New Living Translation, copyright ©
1996, 2004, 2007, 2013. Used by permission of Tyndale House Publishers Inc., Carol
Stream, Illinois 60188. All rights reserved. Scripture quotations marked (KJV) are taken
from the King James Version. Scripture quotations marked (NASB) are taken from the New
American Standard Bible®. © Copyright The Lockman Foundation 1960, 1962, 1963,
1968, 1971, 1972, 1973, 1975, 1977, 1995. Used by permission. (www.Lockman.org).
Scripture quotations marked (NIV) are taken from the Holy Bible, New International
Version®, NIV®. Copyright © 1973, 1978, 1984 by Biblica Inc.™ Used by permission
of Zondervan. All rights reserved worldwide. www.zondervan.com.

Italics in Scripture quotations reflect the author's added emphasis.

Details in some anecdotes and stories have been changed to protect the identities of the
persons involved.

The views expressed in this book are those of the author and do not reflect the official
policy or position of the U.S. Army, the Department of Defense, or the U.S. government.

Trade Paperback ISBN 978-1-60142-692-5
eBook ISBN 978-1-60142-693-2

Cover design by Kristopher K. Orr

Published in the United States by WaterBrook Multnomah, an imprint of the Crown
Publishing Group, a division of Penguin Random House LLC, New York.

Multnomah and its mountain colophon are registered trademarks of Penguin Random
House LLC.

Library of Congress Cataloging-in-Publication Data
McDougall, John (US Army Chaplain)
   Jesus was an Airborne Ranger : finding your purpose following the warrior Christ / John
Mcdougall.—First Edition.
       pages cm
   Includes bibliographical references.
   ISBN 978-1-60142-692-5—ISBN 978-1-60142-693-2 (electronic) 1. Soldiers—
Religious life. 2. Jesus Christ—Example. 3. Christian life. 4. War—Religious aspects—
Christianity. I. Title.
   BV4588.M38 2015
   248.8'8—dc23

                                    2015000404

Printed in the United States of America
2015—First Edition

10 9 8 7 6 5 4 3 2 1

SPECIAL SALES
Most WaterBrook Multnomah books are available at special quantity discounts when
purchased in bulk by corporations, organizations, and special-interest groups. Custom
imprinting or excerpting can also be done to fit special needs. For information, please
e-mail SpecialMarkets@WaterBrookMultnomah.com or call 1-800-603-7051.

To all Rangers and their families—past and present—and especially the families of our fallen. As Sir Winston Churchill said, "Never has so much been owed by so many to so few."

And to my three wonderful children—Lydia, Micah, and Noah. May you come to know this Airborne Ranger and follow him into the fight!

Contents

About the Title of This Book

An old cadence was sung in the Army for many years to keep soldiers in step when marching in formation. Although it is no longer sung today, the first two verses have given me both the lens and the title for this book.

(Sung to the tune of "Do Lord")
Jesus was an Airborne Ranger, you'll be one too.
Jesus was an Airborne Ranger, you'll be one too.
Jesus was an Airborne Ranger, you'll be one too.
Look away, beyond the blue.

Jesus led a twelve-man fire team, you'll lead one too.
Jesus led a twelve-man fire team, you'll lead one too.
Jesus led a twelve-man fire team, you'll lead one too.
Look away, beyond the blue.

Foreword

The warrior soul has always fascinated me. From reading Korean War comic books as a seven-year-old kid, during Army Ranger School, through my tour of duty in Vietnam, and on to more recent visits with the troops in Afghanistan, I have been intrigued by the strength and attitudes of warriors. You can see it in their eyes when the moments turn serious. War is serious business.

And war is most certainly spiritual business. Think of it—the most sacred of spiritual experiences often include the following:

- the proximity of death,
- the service of a larger purpose, and
- the sacrifice of self for another.

All of these are accentuated in combat.

Yet this refreshing book, *Jesus Was an Airborne Ranger,* is so much more than a book on combat. This is a book about Jesus at his daring, rescuing best! And your encounter with him in these pages is likely to leave you changed. As a result of indulging yourself in this book, I believe you are going to:

- love your sacrificial Lord more deeply,
- respect your military more thoughtfully, and
- become a person better equipped to "please the [O]ne who enlisted [you] as a soldier" (2 Timothy 2:4, NASB).

Life is a battle, after all. Earth is a war zone. Whether it's back-stabbings at the office or beheadings in the Middle East, all our pain can be traced, ultimately, to the Adversary of our souls.

Disappointment, discouragement, depression, or divorce—all the "d" words that haunt our lonely moments—are wounds from that struggle. Yes, "war is hell." And the universal cry of the human heart held hostage is for a Warrior-Rescuer who is able to deliver us from the hell of our lives on a war-torn planet. That's why I believe this potent book, initially conceived for the special operations warrior community, actually applies to everyone.

The historical Jesus is the ultimate Warrior and the only omnicompetent Savior. The first hint of him in the historical record occurs in the first book of the Bible. There he is pictured on page one as a wounded warrior (Genesis 3:15). The last picture of him in that same Bible portrays him mounted on a great war-horse, wearing a bloodspattered robe and wielding a sword with which he ends all wars (Revelation 19). First, last, and in between, Jesus is the ultimate Warrior.

Consider this. Scripture describes the mission of Christ's Advent in the clearest of military terms: "The Son of God appeared for this purpose, to destroy the works of the devil" (1 John 3:8, NASB). The modern military equivalent is nearly verbatim—the expressed mission statement of every sworn infantryman is "to close with and destroy the enemy." Descending from the heavens above, our Savior invaded enemy space to rescue all of us held hostage by the enemy of our souls. Jesus came to set us free. Forever.

The Bible is too often discredited (usually by those who seldom read it) as something of a fairy tale written in glowing, superspiritual terms largely irrelevant to real life. This is utterly untrue. God's Word, in both raw and profound terms, accounts for all the painful realities in this broken world. Scripture's heroes are not flawless saints. More often, they are leaders, pioneers, visionaries, disciples, and fighters engaged in very real struggles. Abraham, usually considered the spiritual father of our faith, was something of a military man himself. He "mustered" (a military term and literal meaning of the verb in Genesis 14:14) an entire light battalion consisting of 318 of his "trained men" and ran a daring long-range night operation to rescue family members. The success of his mission would have been the envy of today's special operations units. Moses was a major battlefield leader, as was Joshua and his battle buddy Caleb. David not only eliminated the giant, he conquered legions of his enemies, then wrote songs about his victories, including Psalm 18, where he celebrates "crushing" entire troops (v. 29). David's best friend, Jonathan, scaled cliffs to do battle (1 Samuel 14) long before the boys of Pointe du Hoc did the same in 1944.

Then there is Jesus himself. Too often he is portrayed in the media as some kind of otherworldly space cadet, or a "gentle-Jesus-meek-and-mild" who would cast well as a model for a shampoo advertisement. But you won't find this Jesus in the Bible. As a first-century carpenter who procured his own timber from the hillsides, he was undoubtedly a fit individual, highly skilled with hammer and chisel. And he was most clearly a warrior when he squared off with the ultimate Enemy on that piece of historic high ground. There on Mount Calvary, Jesus stood between us and all that would harm us—the very definition of a competent warrior. He took the blows, shed his blood, and gave his life on our behalf. Calvary, the centerpiece of the Bible to which every biblical story ultimately points, is the scene of the most outlandish combat in earth's history. For every believer, it is sacred battlespace.

It should come as no surprise that one of America's most famous five-star generals, Douglas MacArthur, would be moved to say, in his famous farewell address to the corps at West Point:

The soldier, above all other men, is required to practice the greatest act of religious training—sacrifice. In battle and in the face of danger and death, he discloses those divine attributes which his Maker gave when He created man in His own image.

No, it is no sacrilege to refer to the Savior of the world as a warrior sent from God to fight and pay the ultimate price for our rescue. *Jesus Was an Airborne Ranger.* The Original.

Stu Weber
Pastor; author of *Tender Warrior;* Ranger '67

Making the Jump

Your Call to Be God's Airborne Ranger

Green light. Go!"

At the command, the entire mass of men and equipment inside the C-17 Globemaster sprang to life. Hearts pounding and breathing quick prayers, one hundred paratroopers shuffled toward the jump-master at the rear of the aircraft and the two open doors. Outside the plane, all was inky darkness.

Each man carried a thirty-eight-pound parachute on his back, a fifteen-pound reserve chute on his stomach, a sixty- to eighty-pound rucksack hanging around his knees, and a rifle attached at his left hip. With one hand he clenched a yellow static line. With the other he grasped his reserve parachute. Each paratrooper pivoted at the door, then flung his body into the void.

One of those paratroopers was me. I'd made this jump many times in training. But this night in March 2003 was different. This night I was jumping into combat in Iraq.

"One thousand, two thousand, three thousand . . ." I counted as I plummeted until—*snap!*—the shock told my body that my T-10D parachute had successfully deployed.

In the darkness, I could barely make out the faint glow of our objective—a cement tarmac—slowly approaching some four hundred feet below me. Aside from the pair of tan suede combat boots in my view, the scene looked exactly like the satellite imagery I had studied earlier that week.

Simultaneously, all around me, paratroopers were jumping from other planes. A thousand men were assigned to this mission. Our orders were to seize and control a remote runway in northern Iraq. Once the runway was secure, we could bring in more men and matériel to establish a second front in this now seven-day-old war.

The ground drew closer. Closer still. I brought my feet and knees together, knees slightly bent, and braced for impact. I knew it wasn't going to be pretty. We were all loaded heavier than usual. Inside my rucksack I carried a radio and spare batteries, two mortar rounds, and a basic load of ammunition. The ground flew toward me.

Wham! I slammed the pavement like a brick.

Momentarily stunned, I lay on my back looking into the night sky filled with jumpers. Mentally, I checked for injuries. Finding none, I stood, got out of my parachute harness, removed my M4 carbine from its case, and chambered the first round.

Looking at the landmarks on the ground and the men around me, I realized something that was true of both my location and my calling as an Airborne Ranger:

I was right where I was supposed to be.

DROPPED INTO BATTLE

Soldiers aren't the only ones dropped into battles. You may have never worn combat fatigues, but like me, you suddenly find yourself in the middle of a "war."

- Maybe your integrity is threatened. You face a harmful path, but it looks enticing. You're tempted to cave under the pressure. What do you do?
- Maybe your marriage or home life is a war zone. A conflict lingers no matter how you try to solve it. Days and nights feel chaotic. Dark. Heavy. You wonder where to turn.
- Maybe the bomb of a personal crisis has detonated. The ones you value most lie bleeding and wounded. They look to you for leadership, but you don't know what to do.
- Maybe security slips through your fingers. You work hard to be a good provider to those who matter most, but you just can't get ahead. Your foundation feels unsettled. Your future feels vulnerable to attack.
- Maybe you long for greater purpose. Your days are filled with activity, but to what end? A sense of meaning is missing. You want to do something lasting. Significant. True.

> You may not realize this, but someone fights in front of you and beside you — humanity's greatest Warrior — and he is calling you to join him in fulfilling history's greatest mission. ★

There's good news. Although this world is filled with combat and casualties, you were made for this fight. You were designed for the front lines. *You are right where you are supposed to be!* And you are not alone in the battle.

You may not realize this, but someone fights in front of you and beside you—humanity's greatest Warrior—and he is calling you to join him in fulfilling history's greatest mission. No matter what fight you're facing today, you can win your battles when you follow the Warrior Christ.

My mission that night in Iraq was to seize a runway in contested territory, and we did it. But God has something far more significant and lasting for you to accomplish. In the pages ahead, I want to show you what that is.

MY MISSION

I've been an Airborne Ranger for most of my adult life. I finished Airborne training at age twenty-two and graduated from the U.S. Army Ranger School nine months later. I served more than ten years in Airborne and Ranger assignments, being a part of such famed units as the 173rd Airborne Brigade, the 82nd Airborne Division, and the 75th Ranger Regiment. In that decade of service, I completed more than sixty-five parachute jumps—including the night combat jump I just described—into seven countries on four continents. As a graduate of jumpmaster training at Fort Bragg, North Carolina, I inspected hundreds of parachutes for potential hazards and safely led dozens of Airborne operations. I deployed multiple times to hostile areas, including Kosovo, Iraq, and Afghanistan. I've spent much of my life serving alongside some of our nation's greatest soldiers.

But while I've been an Airborne Ranger a long time, I've been a follower of the Warrior Christ even longer. So it came as no great surprise to me when, while shaving at a bathroom sink in Kirkuk, Iraq, early on November 17, 2003, I heard God calling me to leave the infantry and become an Army chaplain. In the days that followed, God showed me that he would use my experiences as an Airborne Ranger to help me minister to this unique and elite company of warriors. He'd brought me to these units to teach me the language, culture, and customs of this group, so that one day I could be their chaplain.

That's what I am today: a pastor to Airborne Rangers. I'm writing these words while stationed in Afghanistan, surrounded by elite warriors who willingly don the uniform and stand in the gap to defend you and me.

> How do most churches today portray Jesus? He's the tender shepherd, meek and mild. He's the long-haired boyfriend we're all supposed to sing love songs to. He's the bearded therapist who wishes we'd all become nice guys (and we all know where nice guys finish). ★

Over the years, as I've listened to Rangers share their experiences with Christianity, I've noticed a problem. It shows up again and again. Mind you, these warriors are among the toughest of the tough. They're the type of men who walk into their Army career center, slam their fist on the desk, glare at the recruiter, and growl, "Give me the hardest thing you've got!" But here's the tension: it's hard for tough guys to follow Jesus.

The problem isn't Jesus.

The problem is the "Jesus" who is presented to them.

Ask yourself, how do most churches today portray Jesus? He's the tender shepherd, meek and mild. He's the long-haired boyfriend, the one we're all supposed to sing love songs to. He's the bearded therapist who wishes we'd all become nice guys (and we all know where nice guys finish). How could our nation's fighting men possibly relate to such a pale-faced, slack-jawed pretty boy?

Perhaps you've felt the same way. It's not just soldiers who are put off by the image of a wimpy Jesus. Lots of men—and women—have the same reaction.

We've been handed a skewed, sanitized, and weakened understanding of Jesus. Not only is this bad theology, but also it gives us a bad role model. Real men can't relate to this feminized Christ. And they shouldn't have to. The Sunday-school Jesus gives us no understanding of why we're here on earth, what we're up against, and what we're supposed to do. *We need something more.*

I'm writing this book to show a different kind of Jesus. I want to help reclaim who Christ really is, the Christ of the Bible. I want you to understand that Jesus is wilder and tougher than you could ever imagine. And I want to help you find in his story your own life-defining mission. I'm going to use a military analogy throughout this book to accomplish that.

FOLLOWING CHRIST THE CONQUEROR

Does it sound strange to compare Jesus to an Army Ranger? Of course Jesus never served in the military, wore camouflage, or jumped out of an airplane with an assault rifle. I get that. But I'm putting the picture of a Ranger in front of you as a helpful illustration of who Jesus was, how he lived his life, and what he calls his followers to do.

Let's put the imagery in a nutshell: an Airborne Ranger executes daring missions to rescue humanity at the cost of his own life. That's exactly what Jesus does for us.

This is no daytime-talk-show Jesus. This is Medal of Honor–

worthy Jesus! Someone men would want to honor and emulate. Let's see him as he really is—a battle-scarred Combatant who stared death in the face . . . and won.

In his classic book *Mere Christianity,* theologian C. S. Lewis wrote,

> Enemy-occupied territory—that is what this world is. Christianity is the story of how the rightful king has landed, you might say landed in disguise, and is calling us all to take part in a great campaign of sabotage.[1]

I wholeheartedly agree. We are trapped in hostile territory, and our Rescuer has come to save us.

Some will argue that this military talk goes too far. After all, didn't Jesus come as the Prince of Peace (Isaiah 9:6)? Didn't he tell us to turn the other cheek (Luke 6:29)?

Yes! But these lines don't tell the whole story. Jesus was not a bloodthirsty warmonger. But he wasn't a nonconfrontational wimp, either. Against great odds, he defied an empire and changed history. Men and women called him Master. They took his message around the world. They stayed true to him even when it cost them their lives.

> Jesus was like an elite, divinely commissioned Soldier. He was strong. He was on an important mission. And he courageously squared off against the Enemy of our souls. ★

We have to ask: Who was this Jesus . . . *really?*

I think the Ranger analogy can help us get a fresh view. The biblical picture of Christ looks like this: Jesus was like an elite, divinely commissioned Soldier. He was strong. He was on an important mission. And he courageously squared off against the Enemy of our souls. When we recover this neglected aspect of his identity, then we can restore a balanced understanding of his person and work.

I didn't invent this view of Christ. My portrayal of him as an Airborne Ranger is merely a modern twist on an ancient Christian understanding.

As early as the first century AD, the life, death, and resurrection of Jesus were being compared to a great military victory over a formidable enemy. This doctrine is called *Christus victor* (Latin for "Christ the Conqueror"), and for many centuries it served as the primary framework for understanding Jesus's mission on earth.[2] According to this doctrine, the skirmish in the Garden of Eden was nothing short of a military coup. Satan, a chief angel, usurped God's rightful rule as King and placed humanity in slavery (2 Peter 2:19; 1 John 5:19). Not willing to surrender, God dispatched his greatest Warrior to defeat the Enemy and rescue his people (Genesis 3:15; Matthew 1:21). About this great victory, Jesus said, "Take heart, because I have overcome [conquered or prevailed over] the world" (John 16:33). The apostle Paul added that Christ "descended to our lowly world" and then "led a crowd of captives" away to high ground (Ephesians 4:8–9, from Psalm 68:18). In other words, he came to earth to defeat our great captor and take us to be with him.

I believe that as Western society has grown more domesticated and protected from hard realities, we have rejected *Christus victor* in lieu of more palatable doctrines. Now, many view war as inherently evil and peace as supremely virtuous. To suit our sensibilities, we have sanitized the person and story of Jesus, removing any mention of conflict or battle.

If you agree even a little bit with my argument, then you can see that this adds up to a huge loss, especially for men. This messianic makeover strips from Christ anything heroic or noble. The resulting religion is like our new deity—spineless, spiritless, lifeless.

No wonder many Christians feel as if they are just going through the motions in life. No wonder so many men I know don't feel at home in most worship services and small groups. We have lost the man-on-a-mission intensity that drove Jesus to the cross. A boy-band Jesus will never change the brokenness in our world. And if you and I follow that kind of Jesus, neither will we.

> This messianic makeover strips from Christ anything heroic or noble. The resulting religion is like our new deity— spineless, spiritless, lifeless. ★

We need to shove aside the pretty-boy image of Christ. We need to meet—and follow—Christ the Conqueror.

Most men I've talked to, whether civilian or military, are just not compelled to give their lives to a lesser Lord. Why should they be?

Why should *you* be?

THE LIFE YOU WERE MEANT TO LEAD

It's not enough to merely be aware of the real Jesus. A superficial introduction won't do. We need to take another look at the whole amazing story of Scripture. If we do, we'll come to know Jesus as our heaven-sent Rescuer, and we'll understand that our directive is to follow him wholeheartedly—his passion, his purpose, and yes, his heroic sacrifice.

I don't know about you, but the meek Messiah is far too timid to confront the pressing realities of evil that I, my family, and my fighting men face every day. He's much too tolerant to stand up for what's right and true and noble and good. If we follow the wrong Jesus, then we will become like flavorless salt or a hidden candle—completely useless (Matthew 5:13, 15).

Many Christians today have a bunker mentality, content to wait in the relative calm of their churches while enemy shelling wreaks havoc on families and individuals outside. In the military, we give such soldiers the worst possible epithet—*cowards*.

No self-respecting Ranger wants to sit on the sidelines while others do the fighting. On a recent deployment to Afghanistan, my commander made the difficult decision to leave one of our 150-man companies at home station. The average person might have been relieved to avoid combat duty, but not these Rangers! Many were devastated. They all wanted to contribute to the fight.

One such warrior is Private First Class Luke Holtz. After his older brother Tyler was killed in Afghanistan with the Rangers in 2011, Luke volunteered to don the uniform and serve in the same unit. He wanted so badly to deploy and confront evil face to face, as Tyler had. In 2013, Luke got his wish and deployed to Logar Province, the area where his brother had fallen two years earlier. Luke said to me, "I'm only in the Rangers for a few years. I want to make the most of it!"

You want to make the most of your life, right? I do too, and here's my promise to you. As we grasp the truth of the Warrior Christ, we will understand what it means to be men and women of God. We'll find our real identity and purpose. When we follow the Warrior Christ, we will be set free from despair, darkness, and purposelessness in our marriages, families, churches, and communities, and we will be used by God to set others free. Only a Warrior Christ can so positively impact this fractured planet.

In Ranger vernacular, Jesus was a badass.

Are you appalled at the use of that mildly irreverent term to describe the Son of God? Or is your heart stirred at the thought of Jesus being tough enough to merit that label? Warriors use that term, not as an insult, but as a badge of honor! If any soldier deserves that label, then Jesus does even more so.[3]

And we should want the same to be said of us. The church has plenty of lukewarm Christians who honor God with their lips but whose hearts are far from him (Matthew 15:8).

God is looking for true warriors who will trade all that this life offers for the privilege to take up arms and charge the field beside him in defiance of our great Enemy. Jesus referred to this aggressive and determined spirit:

The kingdom of heaven has been *forcefully advancing,* and *forceful men* lay hold of it. (Matthew 11:12, NIV)

Jesus certainly was that kind of forceful man. He calls us to vigorously advance his kingdom—as spiritual badasses—in our homes, communities, and world.

Ahead, you'll find action stories—from the Bible, history, my own life, and battle zones today. You'll find practical teaching on a way of life that works. You'll see Christ's mission of justice, mercy, and ultimately redemption unfold. You'll watch him overthrow the status quo, make all things new, and call you to be part of the mission.

You'll never read the Bible in the same way again. But more important than that, you'll never see your own role in life the same way again. Why? Because the Warrior Christ's mission in the world did not end when he departed this earth to return to heaven. He's still working his will in a world plagued by evil and filled with great needs. And he's using ordinary people like you and me to complete this mission. So as you let yourself be drawn into the Warrior Christ's ongoing mission in the world, your life will take on meaning, worth, importance, excitement, and both higher risk and higher reward than you've ever experienced before.

Jesus didn't lead a wimpy life, as he has unfortunately been portrayed as doing. You don't need to lead a wimpy life either. In fact, Jesus is calling you to the exact opposite: a life that's bold, active, robust. He is enlisting men and women who are willing to enter enemy territory and (to quote the mission of the U.S. Army Infantry) to "close with and destroy" the evil in our world.

This is the story we were created to hear.

This is the mission we were designed to live.

The green light is on, my friend, and it's your turn to jump. It's time to enter the fight alongside the first and greatest Airborne Ranger.

CHAPTER 1

The Great Raid

On Mission with Jesus

I will never leave a fallen comrade to fall into the
hands of the enemy.

— from the fifth stanza of the Ranger Creed

The Son of Man came to seek and save those who
are lost.

— Luke 19:10

Following the attack at Pearl Harbor on December 7, 1941, the
forces of Imperial Japan turned south and attacked the Philippines. Japanese troops rained down bombs and artillery from sea and
air and completely surrounded some seventy-five thousand U.S. and
Filipino servicemen on the peninsula of Bataan.

For months, Allied soldiers on Bataan fought back with everything they had. But with limited supplies and no naval support,
doom was inevitable. On April 9, 1942, Major General Edward
King surrendered his forces. The American and Filipino soldiers laid
down their arms to the Japanese and became prisoners of war.

What followed was pure misery.

For days on end, Allied soldiers were rounded up like cattle and herded inland on an eighty-mile forced march known today as the Bataan Death March. Conditions were horrendous. The sun was broiling. The dust, thick. Water, scarce. Food, even scarcer. If they misunderstood an order (spoken in Japanese) or stepped out of line, men were routinely clubbed, bayoneted, or shot. Sometimes imperial soldiers driving by in trucks would randomly swing their rifle butts or bayonets at prisoners along the road. Many prisoners never reached their destination.

Survivors of the march found themselves in POW camps throughout the Philippines, where conditions sank from bad to worse. The captors starved and abused these men. The sun scorched them by day and insects harassed them by night. Cholera, dysentery, and malaria plagued many. Medical care was almost nonexistent. Dead bodies piled up at the sides of the camp. In these deplorable conditions, men often wished for death more than freedom.

For nearly three years, the POWs on Bataan suffered while their brothers fought in now-hallowed places such as Midway, Tarawa, and Guadalcanal. Slowly, Allied troops gained footholds in the Pacific. But as the tide of the war turned in the Allied favor, a new atrocity arose.

As the Japanese withdrew from the Philippines, they began executing POWs rather than expend their limited resources in relocating them. Many POWs were forced to dig their own graves, then were lined up and shot. Other prisoners, in an apparent effort by the Japanese to save ammunition, were sliced open by a bayonet or sword and left to die. In one documented case, the Japanese forced POWs into a bomb shelter, barred the door, doused the men in aviation fuel, and struck a match.

In the midst of all this suffering, and in the face of incredible odds, there were some who went into harm's way to rescue their brothers-in-arms. I want to tell you one of those stories—and then show what it means to you.

RESCUED

If the prisoners at a POW camp outside the city of Cabanatuan were to avoid being executed during the Japanese retreat from the Philippines, then it would require a daring raid behind enemy lines. The camp needed to be liberated; the men evacuated to safety.

Lieutenant Colonel Henry Mucci's 6th Ranger Battalion was the natural choice for the job. They were an elite group of fighters. Speed and stealth were in their DNA.

On January 28, 1945, Mucci and 121 of his Rangers crossed enemy lines and headed toward Cabanatuan. For two days, the Rangers evaded detection and remained hidden until conditions were set for the raid.

> Could it really be that your life today—
> no matter how ordinary it seems to you—
> is at the center of a global rescue
> mission? ★

Aided by an aerial diversion, Mucci and his men advanced toward the camp and attacked. In less than twenty minutes, Rangers breached the gate, overwhelmed eight hundred Japanese guards, defeated the garrison, and readied the former POWs to move. The rescue was a great success. Five hundred Allied servicemen and civilians walked out the gates, free men. More than seventy years later, the raid on Cabanatuan remains one of the most audacious raids in all of World War II.

If something about this story strikes you as familiar, it's probably because you saw the 2005 film *The Great Raid,* starring James Franco.[1] I've borrowed the name of that movie throughout this book because I want to show you that you're actually in the middle of a raid right now. In Ranger doctrine, a raid is defined as a deliberate, small-scale, and covert attack—typically deep behind enemy lines—where success depends on speed, surprise, and violence of action. Raids are used to obtain information, confuse the enemy, or destroy installations or equipment. Sometimes a raid is used to rescue prisoners of war or civilian hostages.

Could it really be that your life today—no matter how ordinary it seems to you—is at the center of a global rescue mission? Could you actually be trapped deep behind enemy lines in a hopeless situation? Or, having been liberated, could God be calling you to join his Great Raid and rescue others—at home, in your neighborhood, and around the world?

THE RANGER RAID

As a young infantry lieutenant, I learned the art and science of stealth attacks at the U.S. Army Ranger School. For sixty-two physically punishing days, I studied, practiced, and then executed Vietnam-era dismounted infantry raids (pursuit of the enemy on foot) under the eye of our instructors. I got so I could—and often did—conduct these attacks in my sleep.

Initially, we rehearsed raids on small objectives using only a nine-man Ranger squad. Later, we progressed to forty-man platoons, training to execute covert operations in enemy territory using both climbing techniques in mountainous terrain and water movements in marshy environs. Regardless of the conditions, the purpose of the raid was the same: to move undetected to a position of advantage from which to successfully accomplish the mission.

Rangers also train for large-scale raids. If U.S. soldiers need to enter a hostile area to secure key terrain, seize critical equipment, or neutralize a hostile enemy, then Rangers would likely be the first on the president's list to call. Modern Rangers have demonstrated this capability during large-scale Airborne assaults in Grenada in 1983 and Panama in 1989. Furthermore, since the start of the Global War on Terrorism in 2001, Rangers have conducted thousands of platoon-sized raids to capture hostile personnel or seize enemy equipment. Almost daily for more than a decade—in the mountains of Afghanistan and deserts of Iraq—these men-at-arms received their missions, donned their equipment, and completed their assignments under cover of darkness.

As they prepare to go "on target," their confidence is palpable, bordering on arrogance. They are experts in their field, executing rapid assaults with lethal effects better than anyone in the world—and they know it.

As soon as they get the mission, these elite warriors file into the ready room (where gear and ammo are staged) to grab their tools of war. With a calm efficiency that only comes with repetition, they don helmets and body armor and load into vehicles.

Ahead comes only danger, but they are prepared.

Are you?

HOPELESSLY ENTANGLED

Another daring mission is underway, only this one is spiritual, and it greatly affects you and me. The goal of this Great Raid is to rescue us from darkness and offer us true freedom. Since the beginning, God has been at work to bring back his captive sons and daughters from behind enemy lines. And it is by joining forces with our mission Commander that we find our greatest fulfillment and purpose in life.

The focus of this book is on Jesus, whom I call the Rescuer. But to understand why his mission existed, we need to look briefly at the bigger picture of Scripture.

> Since the beginning, God has been at work to bring back his captive sons and daughters from behind enemy lines. And it is by joining forces with our mission Commander that we find our greatest fulfillment and purpose in life. ★

It all started the day Adam and Eve sinned in the Garden of Eden, giving birth to humanity's need to be rescued. When our first ancestors ate the forbidden fruit, two facts emerged: (1) all of humanity was now enslaved by the Enemy; and (2) any hope of rescue would require a raid behind enemy lines.

Of course, you might be asking, "Do I really need to be rescued? Seems like I'm doing just fine."

I get it. Tough guys in particular don't like the idea that somebody needs to save them. On any particular day in this spiritual battle, you and I may not see any guards or feel any chains. Maybe, we decide, there's no need for a great rescue after all.

Disbelief is perhaps the Enemy's greatest feat. Satan continually lies, telling people they are free, when they're actually in his snare.[2] Have you ever seen a person choose what he thinks is freedom, only to become enslaved by that choice?

Say a tough young guy—let's call him Derek—is offered his first cigarette. Somehow saying yes feels "free" to him. He'll shed parental expectations, do what he wants. Derek puffs away and soon becomes a regular smoker. "I can quit any time," he insists. But twenty years later, he has become a two-pack-a-day smoker. He's tried to stop many times, but he's physically and emotionally trapped by his addiction. Turns out, Derek was enslaved by his own free choices.

Trust me, I know you could substitute another substance or habit for Derek's tobacco. All of us know a Derek. In some way, all of us *are* Derek.

I see men enslaved all the time. These men are in the enemy's trap, and sometimes they know it, sometimes they don't.

During large-scale Airborne operations, the likelihood of two parachutes colliding in midair is high enough that, before every jump, jumpmasters like me must talk through collision procedures with the men. Big problems begin if a paratrooper gets stuck in another jumper's canopy or suspension lines (the many nylon cords that extend from the parachute to the paratrooper). Initially, we say the jumper is merely "entangled," meaning that he needs to work himself free. But, when all effort fails, we say he's "hopelessly entangled." Whether he admits it or not, that jumper is in a dangerous—perhaps deadly—situation.

Let me tell it to you straight. Without a Savior, we are all "hopelessly entangled" in sin (see Hebrews 12:1, NIV). We are spiritual POWs, and our captor, Satan, will not give us up without a fight. Like the prisoners at Cabanatuan, we have no hope of escape. We have been ensnared by our own free choices. If we die without rescue, only one fate remains: hell.

Fortunately, from the beginning, God saw our desperate need and set in motion a daring rescue. The Great Raid was underway. I want to show you how this mission originated.

THE PLANNING PHASE

In the early days of this operation, God gave only subtle hints about his rescue plan. In Eden, after Adam and Eve had rebelled, God told the serpent who tempted Eve,

> I will cause hostility between you and the woman,
>> and between your offspring and her offspring.
> He will strike your head,
>> and you will strike his heel. (Genesis 3:15)

And so the Enemy was put on notice of God's intent. Satan might have landed the first blow, but the fight was far from over.

Centuries later, God chose Abraham's family to be his chosen vehicle for infiltration into enemy territory. God told him, "I will make you into a great nation. . . . All the families on earth will be blessed through you" (Genesis 12:2–3). God was promising that the divine Rescuer would come through Abraham's descendants.

A number of years later God narrowed the field to Abraham's great-grandson, Judah, from whose line would come both a sacred Rescuer and sovereign Ruler. Here's how God put it:

> The scepter will not part from Judah,
>> nor the ruler's staff from his descendants,

until the coming of the [Rescuer] to whom it
   belongs,
   the one whom all nations will honor.
   (Genesis 49:10)

Five centuries later, God chose Judah's descendant David to head a royal dynasty. King David was a great man, but God's intent did not stop with him. He had a still greater King in mind. To David, God said, "I will raise up one of your descendants. . . . I will secure his royal throne forever" (2 Samuel 7:12–13). This would be the forever King, the great Rescuer who would accomplish the raid God had in mind.

As the planning phase continued, God sent prophets to deliver advance warning of the raid. For example, through Isaiah, God said, "The Lord himself will give you the sign. Look! The virgin will conceive a child! She will give birth to a son and will call him Immanuel (which means 'God is with us')" (Isaiah 7:14). The Rescuer was coming!

Yet the Great Raid would not happen without casualties. The Rescuer would be captured, tortured, and murdered. The prophet Isaiah foresaw the brutality:

His face was so disfigured he seemed hardly
   human,
   and from his appearance, one would scarcely
      know he was a man. . . .

He was oppressed and treated harshly,
   yet he never said a word. . . .
Unjustly condemned,
   he was led away.

No one cared that he died without descendants,
that his life was cut short in midstream. . . .

I will give him the honors of a victorious soldier,
because he exposed himself to death.
(Isaiah 52:14; 53:7–8, 12)

Without doubt, this divine Rescuer would be an exceptional human being. Not only would he be miraculously conceived and from a specific lineage, but also he would have to possess the intestinal fortitude required to trade his life for the world in the most gruesome way. Israel anxiously watched and waited.

KEY ELEMENTS OF THE GREAT RAID

Why did God spend all this time planning his Great Raid? Because that's what an effective combat leader does. When the timing was right, God sent his Son to earth on a mission to rescue you and me. In doing so, he displayed at least two of the necessary elements of any great raid: tactical patience and surprise.

> When the timing was right, God sent his Son to earth on a mission to rescue you and me. ★

Element 1: Tactical patience

Military operational planners talk about "setting the conditions" for an attack. That means commanders must wait for circumstances to become favorable for success. General Eisenhower demonstrated this during the Allied invasion of Normandy. Initially, the assault across the English Channel was scheduled for the fifth of June, but high winds and rough seas forced Eisenhower to delay the invasion twenty-four hours, long enough for a small break in the weather.

God, too, waited for the right conditions before deploying his Rescuer. The apostle Paul, who enlisted in this rescue mission, wrote of God's tactical patience: "When the right time came, God sent his Son . . . to buy freedom for us who were slaves" (Galatians 4:4–5).

What could Paul have meant by "the right time"? How were conditions set for the Great Raid to be executed? Historians point to at least three circumstances that greatly aided in humanity's rescue.

- *Unified language.* In 333 BC, Alexander the Great and his Greek army marched through Palestine on their way to the Orient. As they passed through, Alexander and company taught the conquered peoples Greek. Soon the whole Mediterranean world spoke a common language. This allowed for the early written records of the Great Raid to be rapidly disseminated in one tongue.

- *Transportation network.* When Rome conquered Greece and became the new dominant empire, the Romans built roads and seaports, primarily for the movement of troops. These civil engineering projects greatly enabled future Rangers, such as Paul, to travel and deliver the good news about the Rescuer.

- *Unified government.* Since Rome had conquered much of the known world at that time, there was a common government throughout the region. This resulted in a relatively peaceful situation among neighboring nations, known as the *Pax Romana*. Without ongoing war—a rarity in ancient times—people could travel more easily, which aided the movement of God's messengers.

A common language, a network of passable roads, and a unified government provided favorable conditions for the coming raid and the spread of God's victorious news.

Element 2: Surprise

Rangers are taught to do the unexpected. They never want to let their opponents anticipate or detect their movements. For instance, Rangers don't travel on easy avenues of approach such as roads or ridgelines, because that's precisely where the enemy will look. Rangers sleep in the difficult terrain, such as stagnant swamps or inhospitable mountainsides, because no roving patrols will look for them there.

Once, near the Serbia-Kosovo border in 2002, I ordered a patrol base (a triangle-shaped perimeter used briefly for rest and refit in hostile areas) on a mountain spur. The grade was so steep that an unsecured rucksack or helmet would quickly tumble hundreds of yards to the ravine floor (which happened more than once). But there was an advantage to our location too—away from roads and natural pathways, we were certain to spend the night undetected.

Look at how God used the element of surprise in conducting the Great Raid.

First, he chose an unwed peasant girl to bring his Rescuer into the world. Isaiah had hinted at this, but no one could have anticipated such a scandalous arrival. Even Mary, the mother-to-be, couldn't believe it. "But how can this happen?" she asked. "I am a virgin" (Luke 1:34). Her fiancé was so shocked by her apparent immorality that "he decided to break the engagement quietly," before an angel told him the pregnancy was divine (Matthew 1:19). In the conservative Jewish community where they lived, certainly neighbors whispered about their seemingly shameful secret. No one would have expected God to work through such sexual controversy.

> A consummate tactician, God surprised everyone by the way he chose to infiltrate his Rescuer into planet Earth. ★

Also, God didn't choose a well-connected religious or political family in the capital to raise his Rescuer. He picked a common laborer and a humble maid from an insignificant village in the rural region of Galilee. Years later, a religious leader would reveal the common antirural bias, saying, "Search the Scriptures and see for yourself—no prophet ever comes from Galilee!" (John 7:52). Again, God broke from the people's norms and expectations.

Rather than take the predictable path, he intentionally did the unexpected and used the unlikely to accomplish his divine purposes. A consummate tactician, God surprised everyone by the way he chose to infiltrate his Rescuer into planet Earth.

A CALL TO ARMS

God took thousands of years from Adam and Eve until his invasion into earth to ensure that everything went exactly right. The sheer scale of this mission—the supernatural rescue of an entire planet—is completely unparalleled. Stretch your mind around that length of preparation and imagine the emotion of a POW being liberated. Allow yourself to become overwhelmed with gratitude for a God who loved you enough to plan such a bold rescue.

And let this intense feeling nudge you to reject a comfortable

Western life and enlist in God's global rescue mission. Rather than perpetuate a cold, lifeless religion, let your faith be infused with the energy of a heart set free. Until we appreciate God's rescue plan and experience the joy of being personally rescued, we will never be willing to join him in the fight.

Next, when you think about how much *others* will appreciate being saved, you will be more motivated to help in their rescue.

When my fellow paratroopers and I drove through the city of Irbil, days after jumping into northern Iraq, the streets were lined with people. They'd heard the vehicles coming and rushed out to greet us, grinning from ear to ear and giving thumbs-up of approval. For more than two decades, these Kurdish people had been oppressed and even slaughtered by Saddam Hussein and his regime. Now, in the joy of newfound freedom, they crowded our Humvees and reached out to touch the liberators. I loved being part of their rescue. I loved feeling their appreciation.

You'll love the feeling too when you see that you've helped the forces of light defeat the forces of darkness in the lives of people all around you.

How do you find your purpose in following the Warrior Christ? Let me remind you:

God wants us to see all of history, including this moment, as a great rescue mission. He's planned for it, and in one sense it's accomplished. The outcome is sure. Yet in another sense, it's still underway. God wants you to be rescued and then join him in fighting for others—your family, friends, coworkers, and community.

Trevor Pearsall was a new Ranger, but he wasn't intimidated by the elite warriors around him. A strong Christian, he understood that fighting for the King was more important than any battle he might face overseas. So Trevor volunteered to be a Bible study leader during his first deployment to Afghanistan. Unconcerned with his reputation, he was not ashamed of the gospel but selflessly led that community through an overview of the Bible. And the relationships that he helped forge in a foreign land have remained strong to this day. Trevor counted the cost and chose to follow the Warrior Christ on the Great Raid. Will we do the same?

The plan is complete. The orders have gone out. The conditions are set. But where do we go from here?

> God wants you to be rescued and then join him in fighting for others — your family, friends, coworkers, and community. ★

In the chapters ahead, we'll look at the stages of the Great Raid that Jesus carried out. Along the way, we'll see what we can learn from the Rescuer about our own service in the continuing action against the Enemy. It begins with infiltration.

After Action Review

★ The whole world is enslaved. How does this play out
   in the lives of people around you? Think in terms of
   both spiritual and man-made bondage.

★ In what sense are you now, or have ever been,
   "hopelessly entangled"? How does individual
   enslavement affect you and those close to you?

★ What difference does it make for you to think of
   God the Father as the master Tactician and his
   Son, Jesus, as the divine Rescuer? For example,
   what new aspects of God's purpose for you does
   this military analogy reveal?

★ Imagine you've been held against your will in
   enemy territory for ten years. You tried to escape,
   but eventually you gave up hope of ever being free.
   What does it mean to you that God would initiate a
   military-style mission to come and rescue you
   personally?

★ For centuries, God has been engaged in the Great
   Raid. In what ways are you called to follow him in
   his mission to rescue people? How do you see that
   playing out in your life?

CHAPTER 2

Incarnation

Invading and Impacting a Broken World

A Ranger is a more elite soldier who arrives at the cutting edge of battle by land, sea, or air.

— from the second stanza of the Ranger Creed

I have come down from heaven, not to do My own will, but the will of Him who sent Me.

— John 6:38, NASB

The propellers of the C-130 Hercules churned the air, and the plane's vibrations reverberated in my head. My heart seemed to beat out of my chest, my hands were clammy, my gut twisted in a knot. But I tried not to show it.

When it comes to jumping out of an airplane, you never forget your first time.

I was a young, supposedly fearless second lieutenant at the U.S. Army Airborne School at Fort Benning, Georgia. I trusted my equipment, my jumpmasters, and my training, but my nerves were working overtime. There is something wholly unnatural about jumping out of a perfectly good airplane, particularly when you've never done it before.

We neared the drop zone and the light turned green. I followed the helmet in front of me until it was my turn at the door. There was no time to hesitate. I took a vigorous step out the door. Gravity did the rest.

The first few seconds felt like I was inside a washing machine. But then the pummeling stopped and everything smoothed out, an immense contrast. No more wind. No more churning. No more vibrations.

Slowly, almost silently, I descended under a beautiful, round, pale-green canopy. For a few moments, my blood pressure began returning to safe operating levels.

Then as I neared the drop zone, my heart started pounding again. At six hundred feet above ground level, the descent had felt slow. But at one hundred feet, it felt like I was screaming in like a meteor!

> There is something heroic about a man who will descend from the heavens solely to set others free. But I'm not just talking about paratroopers. God did the same thing for you. ★

Evaluating the wind direction, I pulled a two-riser slip to counteract my lateral drift. Then . . . *thud*. My landing looked nothing like the ones I had practiced in front of the jumpmaster a week earlier. But as I collected my parachute and moved to the turn-in point, I recalled the old Airborne adage: "Any jump you can walk away from is a good one!"

There is something heroic about a man who will descend from the heavens solely to set others free. But I'm not just talking about paratroopers. God did the same thing for you.

We've already seen that God was planning a Great Raid to defeat the Enemy and rescue sinners like you and me. The first phase of this mission was Jesus's appearance on the earth. He came from heaven to earth as one of us: *God became man.*

If we want to understand Jesus's Great Raid, we need to understand the implications of this invasion. Like him, we can invade hostile territory and become God's representatives in this broken world. As we join Jesus on the Great Raid, we can know the thrill and purpose of being a part of history's greatest mission.

THE INFILTRATION STRATEGY

Airborne Rangers infiltrate enemy-occupied territory by descending from the air and then heading straight to where they are needed. In a way, this is what Jesus did too. In Jesus, God did the unthinkable—he came to the earth and became one of us.

To grasp the audacity of this infiltration strategy, notice how completely different humankind is from our Creator.

- We were all born. God has no beginning.
- We all grow and age. God does not change.
- We must learn. God already knows all things.
- Our strength is limited. God is all-powerful.
- We are confined to a body. God is without boundaries.

For God to enter earth as a human, he needed to limit every aspect of his personhood. Like Superman actually becoming Clark Kent (as opposed to merely pretending to be), it would require him to exchange his supernatural attributes for our human constraints.[1]

Some theologians, trying to describe this incredible event, use a literary metaphor. Picture a novelist who creates a world out of his own imagination and, when the setting is complete, actually becomes a character in his own story. Just think of it: C. S. Lewis walks through the wardrobe and into Narnia. J. R. R. Tolkien escorts the Ring to the gates of Mordor. George Lucas fights the Empire aboard the *Millennium Falcon*.

Once the author enters the world he created, he can't change the rules or walk away from the action. No story rewrites. No editing the plot. He must live within the confines he created—make actual choices, face real threats, and experience genuine pain.

And that's exactly what God did for us!

The Incarnation. That's what we call this remarkable, logic-defying event in which God entered his story. The word comes from the Latin, meaning "in the flesh." The Incarnation is perhaps the greatest of all impossible contradictions come true in one baby boy in Bethlehem.

Every Christmas, perhaps without realizing it, we sing about this amazing paradox. In the famous carol "Hark! The Herald Angels Sing," Charles Wesley put into words this incredible event.

Veiled in Flesh the Godhead see;
Hail the incarnate Deity!
Pleased as man with men to dwell;
Jesus, our Immanuel!

Wesley packed a lot of meaning into a few lines. First, he affirmed that the infinite God wrapped himself in finite skin so that we might see and know him. Jesus became both God and man at the same time—"incarnate Deity." The hymn writer then called the

Rescuer a "man" who lived among humanity (John 1:14). Finally, Wesley gave him the prophetic title from Isaiah: "Immanuel," which means "God is with us" (Isaiah 7:14).

Yet this simple and familiar verse merely summarizes this profound event. No pair of couplets—or even a thousand-page theology textbook—can completely explain this puzzling means of infiltration.

THE STRATEGY SUMMARIZED

My wife and I have three kids, and one of our joys is watching them wrestle with concepts of faith. Each Christmas, they learn something new about the Incarnation.

> The New Testament writers were not philosophers wrestling with the paradox of limitless divinity taking the form of limited humanity. They were ordinary men recording a breathtaking but rational event that they personally witnessed, like you or I might describe the Grand Canyon or the Northern Lights. ★

First, they simply learned the baby's name—Jesus—and that he was special. Later, their mental gears turned as they grasped the truth that the baby was also God. As they grow older, I nearly see smoke come from their ears as they learn that God was both in heaven and on earth at the same time. The Incarnation is as difficult for kids to grasp as it is for parents to explain.

But while the Incarnation has puzzled poets and parents for

centuries, the New Testament writers don't seem to have struggled with it at all. They were not philosophers wrestling with the paradox of limitless divinity taking the form of limited humanity. They were ordinary men recording a breathtaking but rational event that they personally witnessed, like you or I might describe the Grand Canyon or the Northern Lights.

John, a former fisherman, became one of Jesus's official biographers. Like his fellow Gospel writers, John discussed Jesus's birth, but not with stories of shepherds and wise men. Instead, John stared right into the heart of this divine mystery . . . and didn't blink.

> In the beginning the Word already existed.
> The Word was with God,
> and the Word was God.
> He existed in the beginning with God.
> God created everything through him,
> and nothing was created except through him.
> (John 1:1–3)

John described the divine Rescuer (a.k.a. "the Word") who had no origin and who made everything that exists. This Word both *is* God and is *with* God. If that sentence didn't blow you away, then buckle your seat belt for this one:

> The Word became human and made his home among us.
> (v. 14)

That's how John laid it out. No existential angst. No mental gymnastics. That's John's birth narrative, his Incarnation story. It almost feels incomplete. Momentous occasions like this one seem to demand elaboration. Entire textbooks have been written on the mystery of the Incarnation, yet John needed only one sentence. He simply affirmed the Incarnation as fact, giving us no fanfare or details.

The apostle Paul was equally brief in his summary:

> Though [the Rescuer] was God,
> > he did not think of equality with God
> > as something to cling to.
> Instead he gave up his divine privileges;
> > he took the humble position of a slave
> > and was born as a human being.
> > (Philippians 2:6–7)

There it is. Jesus was both God and equal to God, yet he gave up some facets of divinity to become human. No drama required.

For most of us, the concept of the Incarnation is too academic. *Incarnation* is not a word we use in everyday life. We need something more concrete, something tangible. That's where the analogy of an Airborne mission can help.

THE AIRBORNE ANALOGY

The U.S. Army Airborne forces originated in the early days of World War II. After the Nazis successfully used paratroopers to enter Belgium in 1940 and Crete in 1941, American war planners knew that we needed our own Airborne capability.

Major James Gavin took the lead. A West Point graduate and former enlisted soldier, Gavin possessed both the intellect and the personal grit to attempt what our nation had never done before.

An Airborne operation is what military strategists call a *vertical envelopment.* For centuries, commanders have sought to envelop (or surround) their enemy by maneuvering against their flanks, which are often less defended. Paratroopers achieve this effect through the air, jumping behind the enemy's front lines and forcing him to fight in two directions at once—a scenario he is unprepared for.

It is a risky operation since, unlike the stealthy Ranger raids described in the last chapter, Airborne missions are bold and visible, certain to draw enemy attention and firepower. If the supporting ground assault troops can't rapidly break through the enemy defenses, then the isolated paratroopers—cut off from supply lines—will run low on ammunition and be unable to defend themselves against counterattack. For just as paratroopers seek to surround the enemy, they too are surrounded.

In July 1943 this American Airborne experiment was first tested in the battlefields of Fortress Europe during the Allied assault on Sicily. Code-named Operation Husky, the plan was for Airborne troops to jump onto the island and disrupt the enemy so seaborne troops coming from North Africa would have a fighting chance on the beaches. The Airborne mission fell to newly promoted Colonel "Jumping Jim" Gavin and his 505th Parachute Infantry Regiment.

On the night of July 9, 3,400 paratroopers donned parachutes and loaded into 266 C-47 aircraft. After a ninety-mile flight across the Mediterranean Sea, they leaped into the darkness as German anti-aircraft fire exploded around them.

The jump and ensuing fight proved remarkably successful. Gavin's paratroopers cut telegraph lines to disrupt enemy communication. They ambushed German reinforcements and resupply convoys moving toward the beaches. The Airborne experiment was an overwhelming triumph.[2]

After the success at Sicily, Airborne troops supported large-scale strategic attacks at many locations during World War II. Since then, Airborne operations have assumed a critical role in American special operations missions. For example, during the first weeks of Operation Iraqi Freedom, Rangers conducted two parachute assaults in western Iraq to seize key pieces of terrain: a desert runway near the Syrian border and a hydroelectric dam outside Haditha. These Rangers showed that the ability to jump on a target, rapidly assemble, and complete the mission is as valuable today as it was in World War II.

> When the Warrior Christ stepped down from his throne and descended to earth, his mission was to destroy sin and death and to liberate humanity. Our divine Rescuer brought life from above. ★

As a prerequisite, then, all Rangers must complete the three-week Basic Airborne School at Fort Benning, Georgia, before assignment to a Ranger battalion.

- In the first week, students learn about Airborne operations in the classroom.
- In week two, students practice parachute landing falls and are hoisted, under canopy, to 150 feet and released for a simulated jump.
- In the final week, training culminates with five successful jumps from an aircraft in flight, which earns students the coveted silver jump wings of a U.S. Army paratrooper.

After jump school, Rangers continue to practice Airborne operations. Depending on the mission, Rangers may jump out of anything from the U.S. Air Force's C-17 Globemaster, which holds one hundred jumpers, to the U.S. Army's UH-60 Black Hawk helicopter, which can snugly fit eight.

But wait, you're thinking, *what does this have to do with the Incarnation?*

Well, the concept of an Airborne operation is to rain down highly skilled and lethally armed paratroopers on an enemy. And so some units have adopted the motto Death from Above. But when the Warrior Christ stepped down from his throne and descended to earth, his mission was to destroy sin and death and to liberate humanity.

Our divine Rescuer brought life from above.

THE RESCUER RECEIVES HIS NAME

I hope you're seeing the bigger picture. The Incarnation is much more than a theological paradox. The word captures one of the most important truths of all time. God *became* human in order to show men and women who he truly is and to set us free from our captivity to sin and death.

When Jesus was born in Bethlehem, according to God's plan, God gave him a name that conveys his unique role as the divine Rescuer. The name Jesus means "the Lord is salvation," or to say it another way, "God rescues."

This name was so important that heavenly messengers delivered the moniker to both earthly parents. An angel announced to Mary the miraculous conception and the child's name (Luke 1:28, 30–31). Later, an angel visited Joseph, affirming the divine nature of Mary's pregnancy and stating what the boy should be called (Matthew 1:20–21). The angel's message to Joseph even linked this all-important name with the child's future mission: to "save his people."

And yet this name choice has even more significance than just its meaning.

The name Jesus also points to an Old Testament hero: the warrior Joshua.[3] As a young man, Joshua was a scout on a forty-day long-range reconnaissance patrol of Canaan (Numbers 13:16–25). Later, he was the general who led Israel to conquer the Promised Land (Joshua 6, 8, 10). Of all the heroes to whom God could have linked his Son, he chose perhaps the nation's greatest military leader. By giving him the name Jesus, God ensured that every time someone spoke his name, they declared his purpose: to rescue humanity.

Finally, God made known the Rescuer's arrival to Jesus's contemporaries. In the military, this is known as *adjacent unit coordination*. In a combat situation, commanders notify nearby units of a pending mission so that they can respond accordingly. In the same way, God wanted people on the left and right flank to know exactly what was taking place in Bethlehem.

On the left flank were shepherds, Israel's poorest class of people. Despite their low standing, God coordinated with them in a miraculous way, using an angel lieutenant to announce the good news of Jesus's birth (Luke 2:8–11).

On the right flank were the Eastern Magi. They were learned foreigners—the exact opposite of shepherds. But God moved the heavens to let these "wise men" know of the Rescuer's arrival (Matthew 2:1–12).

I love that God announced the Rescuer's long-awaited arrival to such opposite groups. It shows that he would not be a King for the elite alone, nor a Savior for only the poor. And though he was a Jew, he would not benefit just one ethnic group. He came willing to rescue all people, everywhere—no exceptions.

JESUS'S VERTICAL ENVELOPMENT

Have you thought of Christmas mostly as a time for kids to get presents and families to feel cozy? As endless weeks of cheesy music on the radio and bad sweaters in the mall? As the time of year you enjoy way too many plates of cookies and cups of eggnog?

I hope you're seeing that the real story of Christmas is not about any of those things. I want you to realize that Christmas Eve celebrates the night when God's bold invasion of earth began. But to complete the analogy of an Airborne operation, we must see how Jesus fulfilled the strategic concept of vertical envelopment.

The Incarnation was "vertical" in that Jesus descended from above. Throughout Scripture, God's dwelling place—his tactical operations center (TOC)—is described as higher than earth. Moses told the Israelites, "The LORD is God in heaven above and on the earth below" (Deuteronomy 4:39, NIV). Arguing with Jewish leaders, Jesus said, "You are from below; I am from above. You belong to this world; I do not" (John 8:23).

> Christmas Eve celebrates the night when God's bold invasion of earth began. ★

Jesus identified the purpose of his Airborne assault. He told his disciples, "I have come down from heaven not to do my will but to do the will of him who sent me" (John 6:38, NIV). To those who saw him as a pacifist, Jesus said, "Do you think I have come to bring peace to the earth? No, I have come to divide people against each other!" (Luke 12:51). And again, "I did not come to bring peace, but a sword" (Matthew 10:34, NIV). Like an Airborne Ranger, Jesus descended from above, hit the ground, put his weapon into operation, and started his tactical mission.

The Incarnation was an "envelopment" in that Jesus went behind enemy lines and confronted Satan on his own turf. Scripture calls Satan "the god of this age" (2 Corinthians 4:4, NIV). Three times Jesus dubs him "the ruler of this world" (John 12:31; 14:30; 16:11). Similarly, John wrote, "The world around us is under the control of the evil one" (1 John 5:19).

Just as D-day initiated the Third Reich's demise, so Jesus's arrival marked the beginning of the end for Satan. Once, as Jesus faced off with demons, they cried, "Why are you interfering with us, Son of God? Have you come here to torture us before God's appointed time?" (Matthew 8:29). At a confrontation in another city, the evil spirits shouted, "What do you want with us, Jesus of Nazareth? Have you come to destroy us?" (Mark 1:24, NIV). Clearly, the Enemy knew who Jesus was, knew his power, and knew that his own days were numbered.

Confident of victory, Jesus said, "I will build my church, and all the powers of hell will not conquer it" (Matthew 16:18). The Incarnation—God's Airborne assault—had put the Enemy on the run.

Now what do you think about that infant boy in Bethlehem? Are you prepared to view him as a stealth fighter arrived at his drop zone?

And what do his tactics have to teach you about infiltrating the world?

A CALL TO ARMS

I'll admit, few if any pastors mention vertical envelopment during Christmas Eve services. Even for you, the shift between cuddly baby and camouflaged warrior may take some getting used to. But that's who Jesus is. Every invasion—whether Gavin jumping into Sicily or Rangers storming into Iraq—has two basic elements: leaving a place of comfort and engaging the enemy on his own turf. Jesus did exactly that.

More to the point, if we claim to follow Jesus, then we must emulate his life—even to invading hostile territory! Are we willing to step up and enter the spiritual battlefield that rages all around?

Two people I've known who have that determination are Tony and Jess Martin.

I first met them in the summer of 2007, when I was an intern at a church in Portland, Oregon, where they were both on staff. One thing you could tell right away was that God created this couple to be invaders.

> If we claim to follow Jesus, then we must emulate his life—even to invading hostile territory! ★

Tony was the son of missionaries in Ghana. He grew up with two great loves—a love of God and a love for God's people, especially those overseas who have not yet heard God's rescue story.

Jess grew up in Boise with a heart to do God's work. In college, she studied global and urban ministries. In the summer after her sophomore year, she served a two-month mission trip in Ghana, where she met Tony.

It was clear from the beginning that God had big things in store for this couple. They patiently and faithfully served for nearly ten years in Portland, but all the while, their hearts longed to be serving God's people in a foreign land. Invasion was in their spiritual DNA.

Finally, in 2014, with three young children in tow, Tony and Jess realized their hearts' dream. They are now serving in a restricted-access country of Central Asia. Far from the hipsters of the Pacific Northwest, they are loving and serving the mostly Muslim community of this impoverished nation. They know that the road ahead will not be easy, but they are committed. They are invaders and they want the good news of God's Rescuer to invade the hearts and lives of hurting people.

Just as he did with the Martins, God is calling you to invade enemy territory. This certainly doesn't mean that you will become a missionary in a foreign country, as it did for Jess and Tony. (Though it might.)

For you, that might mean striking up a meaningful conversation with a coworker or neighbor going through a rough time.

Or forgiving a family member who has wronged you.

Or volunteering at a local shelter or school.

Or being a mentor to a young man without a father.

Or getting involved in social causes that matter to you, or arguing for business integrity at a staff meeting, or moving into a disadvantaged neighborhood where you can make a difference through living shoulder to shoulder with the residents.

Whatever it is, if you are a Christ follower, he wants to use you to spread his influence in a world that is lost without him. You won't be on your own. He promises to be with you in the fight (Matthew 28:20).

The question is not what you will do or where you will go but whether you are willing to invade as Christ did. Will you step into the fray in the service of the King?

———

His miraculous birth was only the beginning. Next, after thirty years undercover, the Warrior Christ emerged to face off against the Enemy of our souls.

After Action Review

★ Every Christmas, we see Nativity scenes with a helpless baby in the manger. How does the invasion picture change your thoughts about Christmas and challenge the cultural images of a cuddly baby?

★ If you are a parent, then you probably spent a lot of time choosing your child's name. Why is it important that God named his Son "God rescues" in an apparent reference to the warrior Joshua? What difference does this make in your thoughts about Jesus?

★ As God prepared for invasion, he coordinated with poor Jewish shepherds and wealthy Persian kings. Are there any limits on who Jesus came to rescue? What does that mean for you?

★ An initial invasion is always vulnerable to a counter-attack. Did you know that a military force sought to destroy the Warrior Christ soon after his birth? It's true (Matthew 2:16–20). Satan too wanted the infant destroyed (Revelation 12:4). What does this say about the threat that Jesus posed to both human kings and spiritual powers?

★ As we emulate the Rescuer, we participate in his global rescue mission. Where is God calling you to step out of your comfort zone and invade? At home? At work? In your community?

CHAPTER 3

Temptation

Facing Off Against the Enemy of Your Soul

I will always keep myself mentally alert, physically
strong, and morally straight.

— from the third stanza of the Ranger Creed

For forty days and forty nights he fasted and became
very hungry.

— Matthew 4:2

I was tired, hungry, and cold. I huddled with forty other students in
my platoon for some semblance of warmth, our collective breath
coalescing into a giant, misty cloud above our heads. We were waiting for our Ranger instructor (RI) to give us our assignments for that
day's patrol. Some of my peers dropped their heads for a few seconds
of illicit sleep as my thoughts began to wander . . .

Halfway through Ranger School, I hardly recognized myself.
My hair was closely cropped to my scalp. I had lost twenty pounds.
All the upper-body muscle tone that I had worked so hard to develop
had shifted to my shoulders and legs. (My resourceful body knew

that I didn't need large pectorals or biceps to carry a fifty-pound pack for six to ten miles each day.) The blisters on my feet had turned to calluses, and there wasn't a square inch on either hand without a cut or abrasion.

I snapped out of my daze as the RI started rattling off roster numbers.

Please don't let him call 180, I prayed silently. *Please, please don't let him call me.*

Getting your number called meant you would be a leader on the upcoming mission. Besides the stress of being graded, serving as leader is more mentally and physically taxing than being a mere rifleman. And I was already taxed. I didn't want to let my unit down, but I certainly could have used a break.

The RI cleared his throat and called out, "Roster number one eight zero—platoon sergeant!"

That was me. I was in for another long day.

Have you ever found yourself in a vulnerable position? Maybe not at Ranger School, but undoubtedly you've needed to lead when you were physically and mentally exhausted. Or complete yet another task when you were already overwhelmed. Or make tough personal choices when you already felt defeated.

Maybe you're in that situation now. If so, this chapter is for you. If you're not in the military, you might want to swap out Ranger School for something like, oh, the School of Hard Knocks. Same insights apply—trust me. In the next few pages we're going to look at what's at stake when we find ourselves facing a fiery trial—and what we need to do to make it through.

Sometimes we feel that God doesn't understand our struggles. We doubt whether we have the grit to make it through the trial unscathed. But, as we'll see in this chapter, Jesus went through his own

Ranger School experience—and graduated with honors. From him, you and I can learn how to overcome the trials and temptations we face in our lives.

ENTERING THE CRUCIBLE

The U.S. Army Ranger School officially began in January 1952, at the height of the Korean War. It was a fifty-nine-day voluntary program to prepare young combat leaders for battle overseas.

The school taught covert tactics and techniques through a series of mock combat patrols. Each patrol was observed by Ranger cadre, and each patrol leader was graded. Only those who demonstrated the tactical and technical proficiency required to be deemed Rangers would pass. Those who lacked such prowess would be sent home. It was no-excuse leadership in purest form.

Ask Ranger graduates from any era about their experiences, and all will tell similar stories. They endured long periods of hunger and sleep deprivation. Adverse weather conditions pushed them to their physical and mental limits. One minute they were wet and violently shivering, the next, hot and profusely sweating.

In May 1995, the U.S. Army Ranger School formalized its training program into three twenty-day phases.

- Benning Phase takes place at the infantry home in Fort Benning, Georgia. It focuses on physical and mental toughness. Students also learn squad-level leadership (nine men) and patrolling techniques.
- In Mountain Phase, students use rope and climbing techniques to negotiate the Appalachians of northern Georgia, advancing to forty-man platoon patrols.
- Finally, in Florida Phase, students master small-boat

movements and water-crossing techniques, culminat-
ing with a nine-day field exercise in the swamps near
Eglin Air Force Base.

In every phase, the RIs assign students to rotating leadership positions, giving each a mission to accomplish: a raid, ambush, or reconnaissance. Each day, students develop and disseminate plans, conduct tactical movements, execute missions in darkness, and exfiltrate to preplanned hide sites. The cycle repeats until all students have been graded in a variety of duty positions. The pressure of grading puts extra stress on already difficult tasks.

To further simulate combat, Ranger students get minimal food and sleep. This deprivation is important because it allows the cadre to observe leaders and platoons in extremely challenging conditions and allows each student to see how far he can go—physically and mentally—without breaking. Many people never know their limits because they have never been pushed that far. But every Ranger graduate knows how far his body and mind can take him, and he can draw on that knowledge in combat.

Ranger School is an important rite of passage in Airborne infantry and Ranger units. Those who earn the right to wear the black-and-gold Ranger tab on their uniforms are recognized as strong, capable leaders and are often selected for key leadership positions. So important is this school that some Ranger leaders, drawing from an old Spartan saying about death before dishonor, tell subordinates simply, "Come back *with* your tab or *on* it!"

Graduation from Ranger School is required for leaders in the Ranger regiment and in many Airborne infantry units. As a new infantry lieutenant headed to the 173rd Airborne Brigade, I heard in no uncertain terms, "Graduate, or we will amend your orders. You can't lead Sky Soldiers without the tab."

I took that to heart. If I wanted to command the nation's best, then I needed to first be refined in the fire. There are no shortcuts to leadership in these elite organizations. I first needed to prove my mettle in Ranger School.

Fortunately, Rangers do not face this strenuous training regimen alone. From day one, each student is paired with a "Ranger buddy" for support during the long weeks of exercises and evaluations. By design, the buddy team is inseparable. They eat, march, and train together and, in the field, even share a two-man foxhole.

> If I wanted to command the nation's best, then I needed to first be refined in the fire. ★

My Ranger buddy was Air Force Staff Sergeant Kevin Vance. Kevin was the "hungry Ranger" and I was the "sleepy Ranger," so we balanced each other well. Every time we opened a meal, ready-to-eat (MRE), we shared the contents so Kevin felt like he was eating more often. On more occasions than I can count, my Ranger buddy kept me awake during important maneuvers. We wanted to see each other graduate because we knew that his success and my success were intertwined. After two tough months side by side with Kevin, I was honored to stand next to him as we pinned on our tabs and graduated together.

I look back on Ranger School as a crucible: an extremely demanding physical and emotional furnace where dross is burned off and a student is refined into a Ranger leader, equipped for battles ahead.

I can guarantee that you are either in the crucible of testing right now or you will be soon. Life is just like that—no exceptions.

In this chapter, we're going to see how Jesus faced the challenge of intense temptation. After forty days in the desert, he found himself locked in a punishing physical and spiritual sparring match. Through every test, he proved his readiness and further prepared himself for his life of ministry and sacrifice.

If we pay attention, we can learn from the Warrior Christ how to face and overcome the attacks we encounter today.

EXPOSED TO FIRE

As Jesus initiated his mission, God led him into the wilderness to be tested (Matthew 4:1). There he fasted for forty days. Hungry, exhausted, and exposed, he was suddenly in the crosshairs of the Enemy.

Satan loaded his best three cartridges in his magazine, racked the first round, and took aim. The success of the Great Raid depended on the outcome of this duel. I want to show you the battle that ensued because it has so much to teach us about our own battles. Satan doesn't have any new tricks today. The same type of attack he used against the Warrior Christ is aimed at us.

Watch how Jesus won.

Round 1: God's provision questioned

The Deceiver aimed right for the stomach. He knew that after forty days of fasting, Jesus was hungry. Satan also knew that while Jesus could perform miracles, he could only do what was consistent with his mission (what his Commander permitted). So Satan tempted Jesus to go off mission, whispering, "If you are the Son of God, tell these stones to become loaves of bread" (Matthew 4:3).

This tactic hit from two angles. First, it challenged Jesus's divine identity. Imagine someone saying to you, "If you really are a Ranger, prove it!" or "If you're a black belt, then show me!" It would be a threat to your identity, right? It would be like someone throwing a strong right cross to your ego.

> Satan loaded his best three cartridges in his magazine and took aim. The success of the Great Raid depended on the outcome of this duel. ★

Second, the tactic challenged Jesus's basic needs. Fully human, he experienced real hunger pangs, just like ours. Satan wanted Jesus to believe that somehow God had failed to provide for him and therefore to decide to take matters into his own hands.

Ranger students are notoriously hungry. Portions of the MRE that normally they would not touch suddenly become delicacies to calorie-deprived warriors. An informal list of Ranger recipe concoctions passes along orally, designed to get every possible calorie out of the MRE. For example, I downed my fair share of "Ranger pudding"—cocoa mix, powdered creamer, sugar, water, and crushed crackers for texture. Many times, if I could have, I'm sure I would have turned rocks into bread!

Would Jesus fall? Would he break the rules to satisfy a need?

"No!" Jesus told Satan. Then he quoted Scripture: "People do not live by bread alone, but by every word that comes from the mouth of God" (Matthew 4:4).

Jesus didn't even entertain disobedient thoughts. He rejected Satan's offer outright. Jesus knew that obedience to his Commander was more important than satisfying his hunger. He trusted in God to provide all his needs, both verbal encouragement and physical sustenance.

Satan's shot to the stomach bounced harmlessly off Jesus's body armor.

Round 2: God's promises questioned

Next, Satan aimed for the head, attacking Jesus's confidence in his Commander's faithfulness. He took Jesus to the highest point of the temple in Jerusalem and challenged him. "If you are the Son of God," he said, "jump off! For the Scriptures say, 'He will order his angels to protect you'" (Matthew 4:6).

While in northern Georgia during Mountain Phase, I buddy-climbed up a rock face. I wasn't a strong climber, but since my eyes were always on the route ahead, I didn't have much fear. Trouble for me came when we reached the top, did an about-face, and had to rappel back down.

Ever tried it? The first step in rappelling—after securing yourself to the rope—is to back toward the cliff edge and look over your shoulder to your partner below. Then you walk backward until your feet leave the horizontal surface and are firmly planted on the vertical. There you are, hanging in space. Without that rope, you'd plummet like a rock. To make matters worse, during descent you must keep looking down at your partner below.

As I stepped over the ledge, my heart pounded with fear. Would the rope hold? Could I trust my climbing partners?

Then necessity and peer pressure took over. I held the rope securely, as we had been taught . . . and just went for it.

My first few rappelling bounds were awkward, but I didn't plummet. Instead I quickly found that I could trust my equipment, my training, and my fellow Rangers to see me safely down.

Before long, I was standing on solid ground at the bottom.

In this temptation, Jesus too was pressured to face a very human fear. We all, at some point, ponder this question: *In my moment of need, will God come through?* Satan attempted to coerce Jesus into backing God into a corner, threatening the Divine to satisfy human wishes or else.

Again, the Tempter began by challenging Jesus's identity, saying, "If you are the Son of God . . ." (Matthew 4:6). Once more, Jesus sidestepped the insinuation that he needed to prove himself. But Satan, remembering that Jesus had used Scripture against him earlier, twisted God's promise. Psalm 91:11 means that God will protect his people in times of trouble. It doesn't mean we should deliberately create trouble to see what God will do!

Jesus caught the distortion and fired back with more of God's Word. "The Scriptures also say," he replied, " 'You must not test the LORD your God' " (Matthew 4:7). Jesus did not doubt God's ability to save and did not need to place himself in danger to gain that confidence.

Satan's shot to the head ricocheted off Jesus's Kevlar helmet, without effect.

Round 3: God's preeminence questioned

Satan chambered his final round. Since kneeling is the posture of worship, he took aim at Jesus's kneecaps.

Satan knew that Jesus would one day rule the world, but first the Warrior Christ would go through suffering. So he offered the Rescuer a shortcut. Taking Jesus to a high mountain and showing him all the world's kingdoms, Satan proposed, "I will give you all their authority and splendor, for it has been given to me, and I can give it to anyone I want to. So if you worship me, it will all be yours" (Luke 4:6-7, NIV; compare Matthew 4:9).

This must have been a tempting offer. Jesus could achieve his desired goal without the physical and emotional trial. With an offer like that, how many of us would pause to think it over? Ranger students often joke about completing Ranger School via correspondence. "What if," they wonder, "we could earn our tab at home—e-mailing patrol plans every day and promising to walk six miles in the woods, while enjoying good meals and a warm bed!" This is essentially the offer that Satan made: profit without pain and glory without grief.

But Jesus understood that accomplishing his mission on earth would require pain and suffering—no shortcuts. And besides, he already knew that all the kingdoms of the world would one day be his, for he is the "King of all kings" and "Lord of all lords" (Revelation 17:14; 19:16). So he would bow his knee to no one but God. Not even to a powerful being like Satan. That's what I mean by the word *preeminence*—God is superior to all others; he alone is worthy of worship.

Jesus didn't waste time considering the offer. He knew his orders and didn't waver. Jesus shot back, "Get out of here, Satan. For the Scriptures say, 'You must worship the LORD your God and serve only him'" (Matthew 4:10).

Satan's shot to the knees only hit the dust at Jesus's feet.

A Leader Worth Following

Satan had challenged Jesus's confidence in God's provision (food), in God's promises (safety), and in God's preeminence (worship). And despite being physically drained, Jesus obeyed his Commander and never doubted the Father's love, truth, or worthiness.

The Warrior Christ passed the test. He entered the crucible and was proved flawless. He showed himself as the only One qualified to be the world's Rescuer—the Ranger School honor graduate—for he alone faced off against the Enemy and won.

That's good news for us: we have a Leader worth following.

Have you noticed that we are most vulnerable to making costly mistakes or opting for shortcuts when we are mentally, emotionally, and spiritually drained? Hungry and exhausted, Jesus had been sent on an unenviable mission. It was as if his Commander ordered him, "Alone and exposed, hold your ground against the best attacks of a formidable Enemy. You cannot withdraw; you must not retreat." These were Jesus's orders. And he didn't cave under pressure.

This chapter has shown you Jesus's strategy for success. He had studied and memorized critical Scripture passages, using them in the heat of battle to defeat his enemy. The parallel to Ranger School—and in life—is so helpful. Rangers have their *Handbook*. All of us have God's Word. And neither book is any good unless we know the contents and put them to work in our lives. We only succeed if we study, internalize, and execute—under pressure—the tasks spelled out in our mission documents.

> Jesus had been sent on an unenviable mission. It was as if his Commander ordered him, "Alone and exposed, hold your ground against the best attacks of a formidable Enemy. You cannot withdraw; you must not retreat." ★

Jesus went through a trial that every human being has faced at some point: temptation. Just as no Ranger leader is exempt from the crucible of Ranger School, so the Son of God did not pull rank to avoid difficulties. Jesus can now perfectly relate to us in our lifelong foot march because he walked the same route and carried the same loads (Hebrews 4:15).

I know he understood a troubled Vietnam veteran who is close to my heart.

Sober Reality

In the 1960s, there was a Navy Seabee who came from a rough childhood. From an early age, he learned to run from the brokenness around him. He ran from failures at school and sports. He ran from the abuse in his home. He even ran to the Navy to escape a young wife and a newborn son he wasn't emotionally able to care for.

But more than anything, he ran to alcohol to numb the pain in his life. During his tour in Vietnam, he was incarcerated on multiple occasions for (among other charges) a "D&D"—drunk and disorderly conduct.

When he returned from war, the trauma of combat and the reality of a failed marriage provided even more reasons to drink. But in 1970 he did two things that changed his life.

1. He made the decision to follow Jesus.

2. He started attending Alcoholics Anonymous.

These decisions changed my life too. Because, you see, this former alcoholic was my dad.

As my little brother and I grew, Dad cautioned us against repeating his mistakes. "Boys," he would say, "alcohol is a mind-altering drug. I woke up in places and I had no idea how I got there. I don't want that for you."

Once, as teenagers, we asked him, "It's been almost thirty years since you had a drink. Do you think that now you could enjoy one socially from time to time?"

He didn't hesitate, but answered, "As soon as you think you've got alcohol beat, you are setting yourself up for a fall. Besides, why would I risk everything just to have a drink?"

My dad passed away in March 2014, nearly forty-four years sober. I'm sure there were days when turning away from the bottle and facing his pain seemed impossible. But he did it. I'm so proud of my dad for standing up to the Enemy and overcoming temptation, as Jesus did.

Only Dad didn't do it alone. He had a faithful God, a loving family, and stalwart AA buddies by his side.

A CALL TO ARMS

You may not have a problem with substance addiction, as my father did, but the Enemy is after you about something. What is your area of temptation? To bend the rules at work? Explode at your wife and kids? Illicitly satisfy your sexual cravings?

You're not alone. No one is exempt. All of us, at some time, have faced the Enemy's schemes.

So, how do we stand against his attacks?

Leaders always tell Rangers heading out on a raid to expect enemy contact. If they anticipate a gun battle, then they will be ready when it comes. If they think the mission will be uneventful, then they may be caught off guard.

Notice how our crafty Enemy's tactics can be defeated *if we are on guard*. Peter, one of Jesus's closest friends, wrote, "Stay alert! Watch out for your great enemy, the devil. He prowls around like a roaring lion, looking for someone to devour" (1 Peter 5:8). Paul said that we are in a "struggle" with forces of evil and need to "put on the full armor of God" so that we can "stand against the devil's schemes"

(Ephesians 6:11–12, NIV). These men understood that we are locked in a great battle with a worthy opponent. We need to respect the threat and always anticipate attack.

> Our crafty Enemy's tactics can be defeated *if we are on guard.* Peter wrote, "Stay alert! Watch out for your great enemy, the devil." ★

Exactly how can we be on guard?

On guard about God's provision

Satan tempted Jesus over material things, and he'll do the same to us. So we need to identify and root out any hints of greed or envy. It is for good reason that God says, "You shall not covet . . . anything that belongs to your neighbor" (Exodus 20:17, NIV). He wants us to trust in him for our needs, avoiding Satan's snare.

On guard about God's protection

Satan will also cause us to question whether God will keep us safe. But the truth is, only in obedience do we find true security. Sound unrealistic? For inspiration, take a look at the stories of Daniel and his friends. Daniel obeyed God and willingly submitted to the lions' den (Daniel 6), but he escaped without a scratch. His three friends refused to worship a statue and accepted their fate in the fiery furnace (Daniel 3). All were spared.

On guard about God's preeminence

Only God is deserving of worship. When I sin, I may chase after a variety of things, but the end goal is always the same: to bring honor, glory, and pleasure *to me*. Paradoxically, when we put self before God, we lose. We must worship God and him alone.

Many Rangers have told me that they "believe in God." I respond that merely acknowledging that God exists is not enough. Even the demons do that (James 2:19)!

True biblical belief is surrender to God's call on our lives and confidence in his character—that he is good and that we can trust him. This is what putting God first—making him preeminent—in our lives looks like.

On guard with God's Word

Of the six pieces of spiritual armor listed in Scripture, only one is an offensive weapon: "the sword of the Spirit, which is the word of God" (Ephesians 6:17). Jesus skillfully wielded this weapon in his duel with Satan, and so must we. Like a bank teller identifying a counterfeit bill, we must know God's truth so we won't be fooled by the "father of lies" and his deceitful schemes (John 8:44).

On guard for one another

Remember Kevin Vance? He was the Air Force staff sergeant I told you about at the start of this chapter. I couldn't have made it through my "wilderness" experience in Ranger School without him. He would say the same thing about me, I'd guess.

Which leads to one final thought. You and I need to lock arms with other spiritual Rangers willing to stand with us in a firefight. Think of it like this: When a group of soldiers pull 360-degree security, each rifleman is assigned a sector of fire—say a 60-degree arc to his front. He must rely on the other men in his element to cover his flanks and his rear. When one man runs low on ammo, he has brothers-in-arms to his left and right to toss him a magazine.

We need the same in spiritual battles.

Jesus was tasked to face the Enemy alone, but he did so that we wouldn't have to. And none of us should attempt such a feat. Our Adversary has picked off far too many "Lone Rangers" who thought they could do the Christian life by themselves. We need the humility to lean on others in this fight.

Find a Ranger buddy (or two or three). Tell him that you are ready to invade enemy territory and ask if he will fight by your side. As Scripture says,

> Though one may be overpowered,
>   two can defend themselves.
>   (Ecclesiastes 4:12, NIV)

———

The training is over. Jesus is humanity's honor grad. Now he pulls out the operations order from his Commander and prepares to execute the Great Raid.

After Action Review

★ Satan offered Jesus a shortcut to achieve his desired goals—profit without pain and glory without grief. In what areas of your life are you tempted to choose the easy way over the right way? What usually results from taking shortcuts?

★ We may see Jesus as invincible and the temptation as a mere exercise. How does the Ranger School metaphor change that perspective? Does it make Jesus more human? More vulnerable? More relatable?

★ What does it mean to you that Jesus went through the same trials we go through (Hebrews 4:15)? How might it change the way you pray during a trial or temptation (v. 16)?

★ Which of the three temptations that Jesus faced (question God's provision, God's protection, or God's preeminence) do you struggle with the most? What will you do to counter that threat?

★ If you want to go on the offensive into enemy territory, you can't go alone. Who are your Ranger buddies? If you can't identify any, what are some attributes you will look for in a Ranger buddy?

CHAPTER 4

Commission

What God Wants You to Do in the World

My courtesy to superior officers . . . shall set the
example for others to follow.

— from the fourth stanza of the Ranger Creed

I can do nothing on my own. . . . I carry out the will
of the one who sent me, not my own will.

— John 5:30

O n a Saturday afternoon in May 2000, I stood on a football field
with fellow cadets in our blue-gray full dress coats with rows of
brass buttons, white starched trousers, and highly polished black
dress shoes. At the command "Class dismissed," nearly a thousand
white service caps soared into the air.

I had graduated from the United States Military Academy at
West Point.

Later that day, as I stood with friends and family on a bluff
overlooking the school grounds, I raised my right hand and took the
oath of a U.S. Army officer. Before my parents pinned a gold bar

(signifying my new rank as a second lieutenant) on each shoulder, I swore to "support and defend the constitution of the United States against all enemies, foreign and domestic." (Sixteen months later, when the 9/11 attacks happened, I came to fully appreciate what those words meant!) I further promised, with God's help, to "well and faithfully discharge the duties of the office upon which I am about to enter." With those words, my journey from high school soccer player to U.S. Army infantry lieutenant was complete. After four years of rigorous training, I was finally commissioned.

> Following Jesus is about so much more than a choice we've made or a way of life we aspire to. Jesus has passed his authority to you and me for a specific mission — to finish the work he began. ★

In this chapter, I want to show you that following Jesus is about so much more than a choice we've made or a way of life we aspire to. We will see that Jesus was divinely commissioned—set apart and authorized—by God for his ministry on earth. And we'll see what that means for his followers. Jesus has passed that authority to you and me for our specific mission—to finish the work he began.

COMMISSIONING RANGERS

You might be wondering why a commission even matters. Why couldn't followers of Christ just get after it on our own? Why the need for a higher authority, a greater power? And what does swearing to fulfill solemn duties and sacred responsibilities have to do with following the Warrior Christ?

That's where the Ranger story can help.

In 1974, our nation was coming out of a decade of costly combat in Vietnam, and the Army chief of staff, General Creighton Abrams, recognized the need for a unit of elite troops to be the standard bearers for an exhausted and demoralized army. Facing widespread crime, drug use, and general indiscipline within the ranks, Army leaders created a change agent to help turn around the beleaguered culture of the force.

Drawing on their proud lineage from the Second World War, General Abrams reactivated two U.S. Army Ranger battalions. When Lieutenant Colonel Kenneth Leuer was selected to command the 1st Battalion, General Abrams personally met with him to give clear intent as to the mission of these Ranger battalions. His verbal guidance was later codified in what came to be known as the Abrams Charter. It provided a threefold vision for these newly formed Ranger battalions.

- First, General Abrams wanted an exceptional fighting force that would set the standard for tactical competence and technical expertise.
- Second, knowing a Ranger battalion had potential to become the breeding ground for well-trained and well-armed bullies, he instructed that the battalion be disbanded if that happened.
- Finally, he envisioned that this unit would be a beacon of excellence to the rest of the U.S. Army and the war-weary American public.

Abrams's clear and concise intent was rapidly executed, and the

1st Ranger Battalion was reactivated eight months later, on August 22, 1974. Four decades and many conflicts later, the Abrams Charter still drives the purpose and mission of today's 75th Ranger Regiment.

Rangers need a clear mission if they are to achieve their commander's intent. Today, every mission begins with an operations order (OPORD). It's an established format communicating both what must be done (the mission) and how it's to be completed (the intent). In five concise paragraphs, the commander states what he wants to achieve during a given mission:

1. *Situation*—provides the status and location of both friendly and enemy forces
2. *Mission*—gives the task and purpose for the operation
3. *Execution*—details how the mission will be completed, from start to finish
4. *Service and Support*—lists resources available for the mission
5. *Command and Signal*—identifies the leaders and the communications plan

Altogether, the five-paragraph OPORD provides the framework to ensure that the leader covers every critical detail of the mission, so subordinates thoroughly understand the plan.

Now let's apply this to our analogy of Jesus as an Airborne Ranger, sent from heaven.

God's Operations Order

It doesn't take much to see that God also provided the Warrior Christ with an OPORD for the Great Raid. Seven centuries before Jesus walked the earth, God previewed the Rescuer's mission to the prophet Isaiah.

After his baptism and temptation in the desert, Jesus traveled throughout the fishing villages near where he grew up and began to spread the news of his campaign on earth. Returning to his hometown of Nazareth, Jesus went to the local synagogue, as was his custom (Luke 4:16). He stood before the assembly and read from Isaiah 61:1–2 concerning his five-part mission on earth:

> The Spirit of the LORD is upon me,
>> for he has anointed me to bring Good News to
>> the poor.
> He has sent me to proclaim that captives will be
>> released,
>> that the blind will see,
> that the oppressed will be set free,
>> and that the time of the LORD's favor has come.
>> (Luke 4:18–19)

The first line alerts the listener that the coming Rescuer would have the "Spirit of the LORD." In the Old Testament, this phrase is often used to describe the gift given to God's chosen leaders: warriors like Gideon and Samson, kings like Saul and David, and prophets like Ezekiel and Micah.[1] Therefore, the people could accurately infer that this coming Rescuer would be a Warrior-King who would deliver God's message.

If the phrase "Spirit of the LORD" was not enough, God added the word "anointed" so people would know for certain he meant the coming Rescuer. This term usually referred to pouring oil over someone or something to set it apart for God's use.[2] The word "anointed" quickly became the nickname people used for the coming Rescuer. Both the Hebrew word *Messiah* and the Greek word *Christ* mean "anointed one" (John 1:41; 4:25). The people in the synagogue at Nazareth certainly knew who this passage was about.

Now that Jesus had their attention, he read his five-line OPORD to describe his mission as the Rescuer—and our mission as well.

1. Good news for the poor

Ask anyone in financial distress—the single mom, the unemployed dad, or the homeless person—and see how much they long for good news. God promised that the Rescuer would speak to the destitute and satisfy that hope (Luke 4:18). Jesus demonstrated this part of his mission when he said, "God blesses you who are poor, for the Kingdom of God is yours" (Luke 6:20).

Jesus countered the prevailing belief that only the wealthy were favored by God. This was "good news" to those of humble means. From day one, Jesus empathized with the poor by coming into the world as a mere carpenter's kid and by living the unencumbered existence of an itinerant teacher (Matthew 13:55; Luke 9:58).

2. Freedom for captives

Talk with someone in bondage—whether by prison walls, addictions, or abusive situations—and you'll realize how important freedom can be. God's Chosen One would proclaim release for such captives (Luke 4:18). The meaning here closely relates to being set free from the bondage of sin. The word "released" carries with it the concept of pardon.

Just before his death—using the identical Greek word—Jesus predicted that his life would be given "as a sacrifice to *forgive* the sins of many" (Matthew 26:28). Elsewhere, Jesus said that "everyone who sins is a slave of sin" but that the truth about him will "set

[us] free" (John 8:34, 32). His mission would release those in bondage to sin.

3. Sight for the blind

Try going an hour without using your eyes, and you will realize how critical vision is. The Anointed One would declare "that the blind will see" (Luke 4:18). Jesus fulfilled this concept both tangibly and intangibly. As the Great Physician, he healed those who were physically unable to see, touching them and restoring their sight (Matthew 9:30; John 9:1–7). Perhaps more importantly, like a true prophet, he enabled others to spiritually see the truth about themselves and what God was doing in the world (Matthew 13:16; John 9:39).

Right before healing a blind man, Jesus alluded to both aspects of his sight-restoring mission, saying, "I am the light of the world" (John 9:5). Indeed, he came to bring both physical and spiritual sight to a blind world.

4. Freedom for the oppressed

God's Warrior-King would announce "that the oppressed will be set free" (Luke 4:18). While this sounds similar to line two of this divine OPORD, there are substantial differences. While the earlier line refers to individuals who are "captive" in personal sin, this one refers to groups who are "oppressed" (literally, broken into pieces) by unjust social systems. Another translation could be "downtrodden."

In addition to confronting personal disobedience, Jesus countered systemic injustice. He criticized leaders of Israel for abusing positions of authority, saying, "They tie up heavy loads and put them on men's shoulders, but they themselves are not willing to lift a finger to move them" (Matthew 23:4, NIV). Jesus's passion about injustice led to his destructive outburst in the temple. He called the money-changers and dove sellers "thieves" for taking advantage of the poor who came to worship. He ordered them to stop these unfair practices (Mark 11:15–17). We see that Jesus came, not just to forgive individual sin, but also to liberate the downtrodden from injustice.

Another elite fighting force—the U.S. Army Special Forces—has adopted the motto *De oppresso liber*. Like Jesus, they have accepted the mission to "free the oppressed."

5. Announcing the Lord's favor

Finally, the chosen Messenger would reveal "that the time of the LORD's favor has come" (Luke 4:19). At the time of Jesus, the Jewish nation had been under the thumb of a foreign empire for six hundred years.[3] People hadn't heard from God's prophets for almost five centuries![4] Like POWs trapped in a foreign land, it would be easy for Israel to feel forgotten by God.

> God demonstrated his great love by sending the Rescuer, as foretold, to execute the Great Raid and free us from slavery. That is the extent of the Lord's favor! ★

But Jesus himself was physical proof that the Lord's favor had come: "For God loved the world so much that he gave his one and only Son" (John 3:16, NLT 2007). In agreement, Paul would later write, "Now is the time of God's favor, now is the day of salvation" (2 Corinthians 6:2, NIV).

God had not forgotten the need; he demonstrated his great love by sending the Rescuer, as foretold, to execute the Great Raid and free us from slavery. That is the extent of the Lord's favor!

———

Just as Rangers receive clear instructions before executing a mission, so Jesus received clear guidance from his Commander in heaven. A dutiful Soldier, he executed to perfection the fivefold mission assigned to him in this Scripture passage. As God's Rescuer in the flesh, he announced to the people exactly what he was about to do.

As Jesus rolled up the scroll, handed it back to the attendant, and sat down, he was able to say, "The Scripture you've just heard has been fulfilled this very day!" (Luke 4:21).

Fulfilling the Mission

Not only did Jesus publicly read the OPORD, but he also carried it out. Most of his ministry was about proclaiming good news (lines one and five), liberating those trapped by sin (lines two and four), and restoring sight for the blind (line three). Those who read the OPORD and were looking for the Rescuer saw Jesus's actions and responded in belief.

> When Jesus had finished saying these things, the crowds were amazed at his teaching. (Matthew 7:28)

> The people were amazed when they saw the mute speaking, the crippled made well, the lame walking and the blind seeing. (Matthew 15:31, NIV)

Even as he spoke, many put their faith in him.
(John 8:30, NIV)

Others had their doubts. One unlikely doubter was Jesus's relative and Ranger buddy John the Baptist (Luke 1:36, 60). Although
John was the first to publicly declare Jesus's identity and mission—
"The Lamb of God who takes away the sin of the world!" (John
1:29)—he later wondered if his initial assessment was correct.

John had been thrown in prison for speaking out against the
regional ruler and his immoral behavior (Mark 6:17–18). Meanwhile, Jesus had begun his mission in Galilee and his fame was growing (Mark 1:14, 45). Even in prison, John received reports of what
Jesus was doing (Luke 7:18). But he still wasn't sure if his cousin was
the long-awaited Rescuer: "So he sent his disciples to ask Jesus, 'Are
you the [Rescuer] we've been expecting, or should we keep looking
for someone else?'" (Matthew 11:2–3).

It was an honest question, and Jesus, overlooking their doubts,
referred directly to the OPORD and gave them an honest answer:
"Go back to John and tell him what you have heard and seen—the
blind see, the lame walk, the lepers are cured, the deaf hear, the
dead are raised to life, and the Good News is preached to the poor"
(vv. 4–5).

We don't know how John or his disciples responded. But given
their knowledge of the OPORD, I'm confident that they took Jesus's
words as intended—"Yes, I am the long-awaited Rescuer!"

WINGS OVER ALASKA

My friends Pete and Betsy Ekle also know what it means to be commissioned. And what it means to live out that commission.

I met this wonderful couple at seminary, where Pete was studying to do missions aviation. He wanted to combine his enthusiasm for aircraft with his passion about the gospel. They felt God calling them to Alaska to support the many rural missionaries in hard-to-reach locations.

The preparation for this ministry took several years. First, Pete had to finish his degree. Then he trained to become a certified pilot. Finally, the couple needed to raise the financial support to leave for the mission field.

In the fall of 2014, Pete and Betsy finally realized their dream. But before they packed up their Suburban for the long drive from Portland, Oregon, to Kenai, Alaska, they were officially commissioned and deployed by their home church. "Go into all the world," the pastor read from Mark 16:15, "and preach the Good News to everyone." And that is exactly what they are doing.

A CALL TO ARMS

Many people are looking for direction. They want their lives to mean something but don't know where to find purpose. I've been there. As a young man, I thought I would find contentment in a prestigious education. When that didn't satisfy, I looked for it in marriage and family. My wife and kids are great, but still a piece was missing. Finally, I thought I would find it in a successful career. But none of these things provided the ultimate meaning that I longed for. Perhaps you can relate.

I realize now that our longing for purpose comes from God. He placed it in our hearts, and only he has the means to satisfy it. I suppose that even Jesus—in his human nature—longed for a life of meaning. And so God gave him a clear five-point mission during his invasion on earth. Rangers would certainly see this as Jesus's OPORD—an assignment from higher headquarters that he must accomplish to be successful.

> Our longing for purpose comes from God. He placed it in our hearts, and only he has the means to satisfy it. ★

If you and I want to find the purpose that Jesus found, then we need to focus on the same five things.

I shared this concept with a fellow Ranger officer over a meal in Afghanistan, and he reminded me of a military term called "nested intent." It means that whatever I am doing must support what my higher headquarters is doing. (The platoon supports the company mission; the company supports the battalion mission; and so on.) If a subordinate unit doesn't support the commander's intent, then it is a rogue element, at best having no impact on the objective and at worst inhibiting mission accomplishment!

In the early days of the Vietnam conflict, on November 14, 1965, Lieutenant Colonel Hal Moore's 1st Battalion of the 7th Cavalry Division invaded Landing Zone X-Ray, a small clearing near a large North Vietnamese army camp in the Ia Drang Valley. Soon after the UH-1 "Huey" helicopters touched down, Moore's battalion came upon heavy enemy fire.

One young lieutenant, with disregard for sound tactics, charged into the thick jungle in pursuit of a fleeing enemy. He was quickly killed, and the twenty-eight men following him, separated from the Americans on X-Ray, became known as the "Lost Platoon." Moore directed three dangerous and costly rescue attempts before the beleaguered platoon and its twenty-two casualties were finally recovered.

One officer's foolhardy decision had put himself, his men, and the entire mission in jeopardy.[5]

How do we focus on the Commander's mission? We live the way he did, and by his divine power, we pursue the same mission:

- *We preach good news to the poor.* Some in the church have read this task as only evangelism and others see merely social justice. Jesus made no such division, spending as much time feeding and healing as he did preaching and teaching. We mustn't stop at only half of the good news.[6] My home church, for example, regularly serves at the Portland Rescue Mission, providing workers for both the meal and the following chapel service.

- *We release those held captive to sin.* Too often we condemn people ensnared by sin instead of helping them get free, as Jesus did. We must remember that we once had a "log in [our] own eye" so that we will have the compassion to address "the speck in [our] friend's eye" (Matthew 7:5). Only then will we fulfill this mission of our Warrior Leader. Many churches have started substance abuse and sexual addiction ministries in order that these "captives" might experience true freedom.

- *We bring sight to the blind.* Jesus accomplished this task both through miraculous healing and through spiritual teaching. As his followers, we are called to care for the sick through medicine and prayer (James 5:14–15) and to work with the Holy Spirit to open eyes that "cannot [yet] see the Kingdom of God" (John 3:3). Jesus cared for both body and soul, and his soldiers must mirror his actions. In this spirit, for several years our church has partnered with Haiti Foundation of Hope, providing both medical and spiritual care to the poorest nation in the Western Hemisphere.

- *We set free the broken and oppressed.* The church tradition I grew up in said little or nothing about systemic injustice. Yet Jesus's concern for the downtrodden is evident; how could we miss it? He even said that displaying justice and mercy was more important than fulfilling religious requirements (Matthew 23:23). Many have this backward, and so we must realign our mission with our Commander's mission, showing compassion to the "harassed and helpless" among us (Matthew 9:36, NIV). This is why groups like the International Justice Mission are fighting to end sex trafficking, police brutality, and other systemic injustices around the world.

- *We declare that God's favor has arrived.* Every few months, it seems, some group of Christians makes news headlines by proclaiming that a vengeful, wrath-filled God will repay this nation for indiscretions. But this is not the message Jesus came to deliver! Certainly God is just. But if Jesus focused on communicating God's favor toward a sinful humanity (and not his wrath), then shouldn't we do the same (Romans 5:8–9)? Some are. For over sixty-five years, for example, the people at World Vision have boldly declared the favor and goodness of God to needy people across the globe through both their words and their actions.

If you are a follower of Jesus, then you have been commissioned—officially charged with solemn duties and sacred responsibilities, as I was that day years ago when I raised my right hand and took the oath as a new military officer. You have been granted God's authority and power. And you have been entrusted to complete your Commander's Operations Order.

> If you are a follower of Jesus, then you have been commissioned—officially charged with solemn duties and sacred responsibilities. ★

Only in this pursuit will we find the life of meaning, purpose, and fulfillment that we were created for and that we so deeply desire.

———

Jesus publicly declared his intent and started to carry out his fivefold mission from God, just as the prophecy said. To finish the job, he would need to recruit some soldiers.

After Action Review

★ In the Old Testament, the phrase "Spirit of the LORD" was used to describe a gift given to kings, warriors, and prophets. The act of being "anointed" often referred to those set apart to be priests. Since Isaiah used both terms about the coming Rescuer, what does this say about the person and work of Jesus?

★ What does the metaphor of Isaiah's prophecy being an "operations order" reveal about the relationship between Commander and Rescuer? How is it similar to or different from your understanding of the Father-Son metaphor? (John 5:30 and 1 Corinthians 11:3.)

★ John the Baptist needed more evidence to be certain that Jesus was the long-awaited Rescuer. Given what you know about the divine OPORD, what do you think about Jesus's indirect response? Do you think John was convinced? Are you?

★ Most of us think that Jesus's primary mission was to forgive personal sin. Were you surprised by any of the other four tasks in his OPORD? Overall, how are Christians today doing in accomplishing these five tasks?

★ As a Commander, God wants the purpose of our lives to be nested with his overall mission in the world. Which of the five missions are you currently accomplishing? Which ones need improvement? What will you do differently to fulfill those tasks?

CHAPTER 5

Selection

What It Takes to Serve in Jesus's Squad

Gallantly will I show the world that I am a specially
selected and well-trained soldier.

— from the fourth stanza of the Ranger Creed

You did not choose Me but I chose you.

— John 15:16, NASB

Major William Orlando Darby is credited with creating the modern Rangers. A 1933 graduate from West Point, Darby was the obvious choice for the job. A seasoned soldier and insatiable student of military arts, he took a strong interest in aircraft and had participated in amphibious landing exercises in the United States and the Caribbean prior to the war.

Major Darby was also a natural leader. He insisted that every officer train alongside his men—a practice still observed by Rangers. He wanted every man to know just how hard it was to be the best of the best.

The First Ranger Infantry Battalion (the formal designation

during WWII) was organized on June 19, 1942, in Carrickfergus, Northern Ireland, where the men had been deployed. From the inception of the Rangers, Darby understood that the Ranger outfit would be only as strong as its individual recruits. So he drew from the finest soldiers—all volunteers—of established Army units stationed overseas.

Darby and his officers personally interviewed each potential Ranger, looking for the right combination of physical strength and personal grit. They sought young men with strong personalities who wanted to do something meaningful, to give their all in the fight for freedom.

This first Ranger battalion started with two thousand volunteers. Nearly three-quarters of the men didn't make the cut. The 520 Rangers who did were the finest our nation had to offer—an elite special-operations strike force that could accomplish missions no conventional unit could.

Because of this battalion's success, the Army created more Ranger units. After the 2nd Ranger Battalion was formed stateside, Darby was authorized to recruit, train, and lead a three-battalion Ranger Task Force. Darby, now a lieutenant colonel, again recruited only the finest to serve in the 3rd and 4th Ranger Battalions.

> Jesus's Rangers—including you and me!—are handpicked and sent out on important missions. It all starts with joining up. ★

Nicknamed Task Force Darby after its beloved commander, this prototypical Ranger regiment made its mark in the European theater. After a brief raid into Dieppe, France, in 1942—the first U.S.

combat action in Europe—these units served with distinction in the North African campaign. They added to their legacy during the beach landings at Sicily and the Allied advance up the Italian peninsula. As these handpicked warriors followed their leader's selfless and heroic example, they etched their names in the annals of history.

Like these brave men from history, Jesus's Rangers—including you and me!—are handpicked and sent out on important missions. We'll see that there's a simple two-step process that starts with being a follower and then moving on to go where God wants you to be.

But it all starts with joining up.

WILLINGNESS TO SERVE

No one is forced into special operations units. This is what makes the organization so strong: each man has proved both his ability and his desire to serve.

What does it take to be chosen? To even attend the Ranger Assessment and Selection Program (RASP), volunteers must exceed the standards required of other soldiers.

- The volunteer must be *mentally alert.* He must achieve a minimum general-technical score of 107 on the Armed Services Vocational Aptitude Battery, a mark comparable to minimums for intelligence analysts or admission to Officer Candidate School.
- The volunteer must be *physically strong.* He must score 80 percent or better on the Army Physical Fitness Test. He must do at least fifty-eight push-ups and sixty-six sit-ups and run two miles in less than 14 minutes, 32 seconds.
- The volunteer must be *morally straight.* He must submit to a thorough background check and qualify

for either a Secret or Top Secret clearance, depending
on duty position.

And those are only the prerequisites! The course itself is even
more demanding.

For enlisted soldiers—private through sergeant—RASP lasts
eight weeks. In phase one, students must complete a series of physical
tests to remain in the course, including a five-mile run in less than
forty minutes and a twelve-mile foot march with a thirty-five-pound
load in under three hours. Afterward, they master common soldier
skills: to shoot, move, and communicate better than average enlist-
ees. In phase two, students advance to Ranger-specific skills: breach-
ing techniques, medical proficiency, and small-unit tactics. Regardless
of their specialty—mortarmen, medics, mechanics—all are graded
by the same standard.

For Ranger leaders—staff sergeant through major—the three-
week assessment is very similar. Then in a boardroom-like experience, a panel of senior Ranger leaders sifts through a thick portfolio
of objective data and grills each student for a subjective assessment.
Like a jury after deliberation, the panel reveals its verdict. The Ranger
candidate hears either "Congratulations and welcome" or "You are
not what we are looking for."

Only about a third of students who start actually graduate.

Is it just as tough to be selected for the mission of Jesus Christ in
our world? By some measures, yes. Definitely. But in other ways, not
at all. You see, God doesn't select just the "best and brightest" to join
his rescue force. And he certainly doesn't ask you for your five-mile
time! God seems to recruit common people with normal abilities to
participate in his extraordinary undertaking on earth. That's the way
it was when Jesus was on earth.

Jesus's Ranger Recruits

In the last chapter, we looked at the commission of Jesus—how he received his OPORD from his heavenly Commander and set off on his mission with focused intent, knowing it would cost his life. We then saw how our commission as his followers also brings divine authority, razor-sharp focus, and the highest possible meaning to our lives.

Now I want to show you how Jesus selected and trained his original team of volunteers to carry on the mission. His recruitment and training strategy might surprise you.

> God is not looking for the tallest, the strongest, the best looking, or the most gifted. Turns out, he's looking for the willing. ★

You'd think a mission as important as rescuing the world would start with a thorough talent search, perhaps vetting the entire nation of Israel and handpicking the most exceptional men to serve in this elite company. But the records don't reflect that. Jesus seemed to pick up followers at random as he wandered around the region near his hometown. At first, it didn't look like much of a recruiting strategy. The men he chose were neither the religious nor the academic elite. They were ordinary men with ordinary jobs, much like you and me, not the recruiting-poster Rangers that we might have chosen.

But he knew exactly what he was doing. Those twelve common men from Galilee changed the world forever.

God is still looking for "a few good men" to serve in his

formation. But he looks for different traits than we might (1 Samuel 16:7). He's not looking for the tallest, the strongest, the best looking, or the most gifted. Turns out, he's looking for the willing.

Look with me at Jesus's selection and assessment program as we see it in the New Testament.

First recruits: Andrew and Simon Peter

Two fishermen, Andrew and his brother Simon, were the first recruits to Jesus's special operations mission. It seems that Andrew was actively looking for the coming Rescuer of the world. We could think of Andrew as a part of the military intelligence (MI) branch, always on the lookout for intel on the coming One.

Day after day, Andrew listened as John the Baptist urged people to prepare for the promised Rescuer. Finally he heard the key piece of information he was waiting for. Pointing to Jesus, John declared, "Look! The Lamb of God. . . . He is the one I was talking about" (John 1:29–30). Andrew wasted no time in following Jesus, and he likely asked many questions like a good MI guy would (v. 39). After confirming his suspicions, he passed on his critical intel to Simon, saying, "We have found the [Rescuer]" (v. 41).

Andrew is also the patron saint of Rangers. As the "first disciple," Andrew exemplified the motto Rangers Lead The Way!

When Andrew brought his brother to Jesus, Simon was given a new name: Peter (v. 42). Why? The name means "rock," and Jesus said, "Upon this rock I will build my church, and all the powers of hell will not conquer it" (Matthew 16:18). Just as the infantry is the bedrock of all combat operations, so Jesus made Peter the foundation of his worldwide mission. True to his name, this recruit became the foundational character of the new, rapidly expanding church after Jesus's death (Acts 1–5).

Without doubt, Simon Peter was the infantryman in Jesus's squad. He frequently assumed leadership among the recruits, speaking up and acting on the group's behalf (Matthew 15:15; 16:16; 17:4). Also, we see in Peter the same brash, volatile behavior common among infantrymen. He was the only one of the twelve Rangers to jump out of the boat to follow Jesus on the water (Matthew 14:29–30). He alone wielded his sword and drew blood when soldiers arrested Jesus (John 18:10).

To these two ordinary fishermen, Jesus called out, "Come, follow me, and I will show you how to fish for people!" (Mark 1:17). His words are significant. The infantry motto is Follow Me! The Bible says that when Jesus gave the command, both men "left their nets at once and followed him" (v. 18).

Can you relate to these early recruits? The nets Andrew and Peter left behind suggest humdrum lives that brought them no sense of a God-centered purpose. Without even hesitating, they followed Christ, choosing to become a part of God's larger mission for them personally, and for the world in need around them.

Are you like Andrew, eagerly looking for the next adventure? Searching for an influential hero to follow? Perhaps you identify with Peter—the naturally gifted but unpredictable leader, the hardworking man's man. God is still calling for recruits of all types. The question is: Are you and I ready to leave our nets?

Second recruits: James and John

Farther along the shore, Jesus ran into another set of brothers, James and John, sitting on the beach, mending their nets. Jesus called and they immediately followed him, leaving their father to finish the patch job (Mark 1:19–20).

I think of James and John as the forward observers (FOs) in

Jesus's outfit. FOs are artillerymen placed in infantry units to call for indirect fire support on enemy troops.

Jesus nicknamed James and John "Sons of Thunder" (Mark 3:17), likely a comment on their bold, aggressive personalities. Before Jesus's death, these two brothers brazenly told him, "When you sit on your glorious throne, we want to sit in places of honor next to you" (Mark 10:37). Can you hear the booming of thunder in their words? The forward observer who calls down the "thunder" from a battery of 155 mm Howitzer cannons makes this kind of bold request!

Commanders like to keep their FOs close since they never know when they might need artillery assets. When other recruits were off grabbing chow or a quick nap, James and John (along with Peter) were almost always with Jesus. This happened at the Mount of Transfiguration (Matthew 17:1), the raising to life of the little girl (Luke 8:51), and the Garden of Gethsemane (Mark 14:33). Wherever their Leader went, James and John stayed close.

> God still looks for passionate warriors to join his mission. He wants you to stay close so he can hone your fervor and direct your enthusiasm. ★

One day, as Jesus prepared to go through a foreign settlement, the people there demanded that Jesus and his men take a different route. Irritated, James and John asked Jesus, "Lord, should we call down fire from heaven to burn them up?" (Luke 9:54). Only Ranger FOs would ask their commander for clearance of fire to destroy a hostile compound.

Can you see yourself in these two fishermen? Do words like

bold and *aggressive* describe you? Would you likely call down fire on your enemies? God still looks for passionate warriors to join his mission. He wants you, like a forward observer, to stay close so he can hone your fervor and direct your enthusiasm.

Third recruits: Matthew and James

As Jesus walked through another town, he saw Matthew (Levi) at a tax collector's booth. Again using the infantry motto, Jesus said, "Follow me and be my [recruit]" (Matthew 9:9).

I can imagine groans and eye-rolling from the others when their Leader chose Matthew. They may have been mere fishermen, but at least they were tough, blue-collar men. Matthew was an admin guy! His father, Alphaeus, was no doubt a man of wealth and political connections to have nabbed this cushy job for his son (Mark 2:14). Besides, Matthew had grown wealthy by taking advantage of hardworking laborers. "No way, Jesus! Don't pick him!"

But Matthew got up, left his tax booth, and invited Jesus home for a big banquet (another indicator of wealth). He invited all his well-connected and similarly dishonest friends to meet his new Leader (v. 15). During the evening, Matthew introduced Jesus to his brother, James (also a son of Alphaeus), who likewise enlisted into Jesus's squad (Matthew 10:3; Mark 3:18; Luke 6:15).[1]

Remarkably, these brothers left the comforts of a white-collar, upwardly mobile career path to work alongside the village riffraff in the Great Raid. Matthew and James, then, represent the administrative elements in the Airborne Rangers.

Not every Ranger goes out on target looking for bad guys. There are many logistics and support military occupational specialties (MOS's)—clerks and cooks, drivers and doctors, linguists and lawyers, analysts and ammo handlers. All these so-called "soft-skilled

MOS's" go through similar training as infantrymen but perform distinct and critical roles within the Rangers.

Perhaps you most closely identify with these two recruits. Working in a white-collar business or industry, like Matthew and James, you may have lots to lose—financially and socially—by following Christ. You're not surprised that four fishermen dropped their nets, but it feels harder to walk away from your kind of life.

But what did Matthew and James really give up? A soul-sapping regimen of spreadsheets and revenue charts for the chance to serve alongside Jesus in history's greatest mission. Who wouldn't make that trade?

———

We don't know as much about the other six recruits (Bartholomew, Thaddaeus, Philip, Thomas, Simon the Zealot, and Judas Iscariot). But Jesus handpicked them for good reasons. Bottom line: he seemed to enjoy calling the most unlikely people, who were simply willing to serve. And that's exactly what the Warrior Christ asks of you and me.

A New Look at Old Terms

In describing these twelve men, I've intentionally avoided using church language—words like *disciple* and *apostle*—for two reasons:

First, if you're a longtime Jesus follower, then you've heard these words many times and they may have lost some impact. My hope is that referring to these men as Ranger recruits will infuse their lives with new and potent meaning for you.

Second, if you are not a Jesus follower, then words like *disciple* and *apostle* are foreign—as unfamiliar as an M240 machine gun might be to Martha Stewart. They are only "church words."

But let's break protocol for a moment and see the great significance in these words for those who follow Christ.

What is a disciple?

At its heart, the word *disciple* means "follower." And so it fits with the infantry motto Follow Me, but it also refers to a student, learner, or pupil.

New Rangers are constantly learning. If you find a Ranger private sitting still (which doesn't happen often), he must open the *Ranger Handbook* and study. He's also continually told to learn from the example of superiors. Young Rangers in a squad are told to absorb from their leaders—to be sponges—because one day they will lead others.

Isn't this exactly what Jesus asked of the twelve Ranger recruits? He called those who would listen: "Come to me . . . and learn from me" (Matthew 11:28–29, NIV). And he strongly adhered to the "Follow me" philosophy of leadership. After washing his Rangers' feet— a humiliating act of service—he said, "I have given you an example to follow. Do as I have done to you" (John 13:15). Peter would later write of Jesus, "He is your example, and you must follow in his steps" (1 Peter 2:21). When Jesus deployed his squad in two-man teams, he said they should emulate him:

> Students are not greater than their teacher, and slaves are not greater than their master. Students are to be like their teacher, and slaves are to be like their master. (Matthew 10:24–25)

Jesus could have added the lesser-known corollary "Ranger privates are not greater than their squad leaders, but must strive to be like them."

Did Jesus's disciples get it? You bet they did. In the three years these recruits spent with Jesus, they gleaned everything possible from their Leader. They rightly saw him as "Teacher" and "Lord" (John 13:13). Like Ranger privates, they soaked up everything they could from Jesus, knowing they would soon be called to teach others.

Sadly, many Christians I've known want to learn "just enough." Enough facts to please pastors, chaplains, or other Christian leaders. Enough information to sound intelligent when talking with other people of faith. Enough Scripture to support pet beliefs or lifestyles.

But not the first recruits we meet in the Gospels. Devoted students, they poured over Jesus's words and regularly asked, "What does this mean?" "How should we pray?" and "Who can be saved?" (see Luke 8:9; 11:1; 18:26).

The idea behind *disciple* fits with the Ranger philosophy of mentoring subordinates to become leaders. But there's more.

What is an apostle?

The title *apostle* is traditionally reserved for the first followers of Jesus in the early years of the church. In some churches today, it refers to a handful of spiritually elite ministers. But at its foundation the word means simply "one who is sent." An apostle could be an envoy dispatched to deliver a message or a soldier deployed to execute a mission.

When Jesus sent his disciples out to communicate a message and complete a mission, they became known as apostles.

One day Jesus called together his twelve *disciples* and . . . sent them out. . . . So they began their circuit of the villages, preaching the Good News and healing the sick. . . .

When the *apostles* returned, they told Jesus everything they had done. (Luke 9:1–2, 6, 10)

They started as disciples and became apostles. They left as "students" but returned as "sent ones."

After Jesus's death and resurrection, he commissioned his disciples-turned-apostles with these final instructions:

I have been given all authority in heaven and on earth. Therefore, go and make disciples of all the nations, baptizing them in the name of the Father and the Son and the Holy Spirit. Teach these new disciples to obey all the commands I have given you. (Matthew 28:18–20)

You will be my witnesses, telling people about me everywhere—in Jerusalem, throughout Judea, in Samaria, and to the ends of the earth. (Acts 1:8)

Go. All the nations. Ends of the earth. These words convey the true nature of the new organization we know today as the church.

Christ's first followers understood this. The book of Acts shows them traveling outside their social circles to deliver the victorious news of the divine Rescuer.

- Though unschooled, John spoke boldly before the Jewish ruling council (Acts 4:13).
- Though socially inappropriate, Peter entered a Roman military leader's home to bring the good news (Acts 10:25).
- Though culturally taboo, Philip befriended a troubled Ethiopian palace official to tell him that Jesus was the One he was looking for (Acts 8:27–38).
- Though a devout Jew, Paul stood among idols to reach a pagan audience in Athens with the truth about God (Acts 17:22).

Their missions took them outside their comfort zones to rescue people of every tongue and tribe and nation (Revelation 5:9).

A CALL TO ARMS

I believe you're reading this book because you want to live a life of purpose. You want to believe that your few decades on this planet will make a lasting impact. Some don't get it—they just want to put in their time, no more. But so many men and women I meet long for something more. Our hearts stir at the words of Maximus, the Roman-general-turned-gladiator in the movie *Gladiator:* "What we do in life echoes in eternity."[2]

> Some just want to put in their time, no more. But so many men and women I meet long for something more. ★

My message to you in this chapter is simple: we will find lasting purpose only by first becoming followers, then the sent ones who are taking Christ's words of life to a hurting, dying, enslaved world.

First, we must be willing to step out of our comfort zones and step into a world in need. Sadly, too many churches have become affinity groups, where we hang out with people just like us—same race, same creed, same socio-economic status.[3] We resist going to the "others"—the homeless, the unbeliever, the foreigner—because it feels unfamiliar or uncomfortable. But the heart of Jesus's mission is to go both to familiar terrain and to the ends of the earth. As God's "sent ones," we are called and commissioned to complete the mission, wherever it may lead.

For some, becoming a disciple and apostle of Jesus may mean

going to a distant land. God called Tony and Jess Martin to Central Asia. He directed Pete and Betsy Ekle to a remote corner of Alaska. But for many, it will involve simply walking across the street.

Tom and Meghan Watson are followers of Jesus who are always looking for how they can be "sent out" into the world. While they have both served faithfully in their local church, they wanted to show God's love in their immediate neighborhood . . . and that's exactly what they do. When an eighty-year-old widow moved in across the street, Meghan helped with rides to the grocery store or medical appointments and invited her over for holiday meals. When a windstorm scattered branches and pine cones all over, Tom and another neighbor cleaned up most of the street, including eight other yards. When someone had a broken light fixture on his porch and couldn't afford to repair it, the Watsons happily fixed it for him.

"How do you improve your neighborhood?" Tom asked me rhetorically. "You do it by getting to know each other and meeting each other's needs." It may not be the ends of the earth, but Tom and Meghan are certainly serving God in their corner of it.

I don't know where God may want you to serve—at home or abroad. But either way, he still calls out, "Follow me." He invites us to drop our nets or walk away from our tax booths and go where he is leading. Only then will we find what we seek—a life full of purpose and meaning.

———

Jesus had chosen his men. He was ready to train them for the mission ahead. But along the way, Jesus's background and behavior would provoke the ire of the religious elite.

After Action Review

★ Which early recruits do you relate to and why?
Andrew, the genuine seeker? Peter, the natural but
volatile leader? James and John, the passionate and
aggressive siblings? Matthew and James, the
middle-class brothers longing for purpose?

★ Jesus called ordinary people from every walk of life
to join his global rescue mission. What does that
mean for you? What does this say about the type
of people you will find in formation alongside you?

★ James and John dropped their nets and walked
away from the family business. Matthew, too, left
his lucrative profession and comfortable life. If they
were able to do it, why is it so hard for us to leave
what we know and love? (Matthew 19:21–24.)

★ We must learn about God so that we can emulate
him in carrying out the Great Raid. How well do you
know the Commander? Are you satisfied with your
present knowledge? What steps will you take to
know him better and emulate him more closely?

★ Like apostles, Rangers are sent out to accomplish
their commander's missions. How are you currently
"deployed" (away from the familiar) in your Commander's service? What "foreign soil" (unfamiliar
ground) might God be calling you to?

CHAPTER 6

Reputation

Facing Attacks in the Line of Duty

I will always endeavor to uphold the prestige, honor,
and high esprit de corps of my Ranger Regiment.
— from the first stanza of the Ranger Creed

The Son of Man . . . feasts and drinks, and you say,
"He's a glutton and a drunkard, and a friend of tax
collectors and other sinners!"
— Matthew 11:19

Y ou wanna do what?!"

As a high school senior, I frequently heard this incredulous question about my decision to attend the U.S. Military Academy at West Point. Strangely, the people in my life who made this inquiry seemed to have two distinct reasons.

Friends and family were concerned that the hedonistic Army lifestyle would damage my Christian upbringing. One girl in my church youth group was convinced that I would come home "a different person," by which she meant morally bankrupt. Likewise, my older brother, who had joined the Army at age eighteen, told me there are three habits a soldier can't help but pick up: alcohol, tobacco, and cussing.

My high school buddies had the opposite concern. They were stunned that I would go to a strait-laced military school and miss out on the wild college experience awaiting them.

Privately, I wondered if both groups were right.

> Jesus was more focused on his mission than on what people thought of him. He dismissed the opinions of the religious elite and embraced his identity as a "friend of sinners." ★

Over the years I saw how both portrayals were rooted in fact. Certainly, the Army has its protocol and decorum—parades, ceremonies, banquets, and the like. But there is also a reason that the inventory of every on-post liquor store reads like an infantry platoon roster. Squad leaders are named Johnnie Walker, Jim Beam, Jack Daniels, and Jose Cuervo, and they're commanded by (who else?) Captain Morgan.

One Army, two very different worlds.

Jesus also had two distinct reputations: Some saw him as a holy prophet. Others thought he was demon possessed.

Fortunately for us, Jesus was more focused on his mission than on what people thought of him. He dismissed the opinions of the religious elite and embraced his identity as a "friend of sinners" (Matthew 11:19; Luke 7:34).

As his followers, you and I are invited to do the same—chuck our polished church shoes and get our boots dirty with sinners.

When we do that, we will find that a life of service to God can also be a life of great joy—filled with food, drink, and great friends.

Sound unconventional, even *unreligious* to you? Surprising? Maybe too good to be true?

It's all part of following a distinctly rugged Jesus and taking part energetically in his Great Raid. Being honorable in Jesus's eyes may not mean what some people think. So read on.

FARMERS WITH PITCHFORKS

Speaking of unconventional, meet Francis Marion—master of surprise and one of America's earliest Rangers. Nicknamed the Swamp Fox for his elusiveness, Marion led a small band of raiders and marauders in the marshlands of South Carolina against the British during the American Revolution. What a contrast! A bunch of country boys facing off against the best-trained and most-experienced army in the world at that time. Wisely, Marion didn't try to beat the Redcoats on the battlefield. Instead, using raids and ambushes, he fought a guerrilla war designed to disrupt and destroy the enemy on ground of his own choosing. Marion's story may sound familiar. It was the basis of the 2000 movie *The Patriot,* featuring Mel Gibson.

While the movie fictionalizes much of Marion's personal life, the depiction of his tactics, men, and opponents are accurate. Marion recruited hardscrabble men of the woods to join his militia outfit. At one point in the film, Gibson's character enters a rough country tavern and declares of the degenerate patrons, "They're exactly the sort we need."[1]

That was one reason Marion's opponents in the war—General Lord Cornwallis and Colonel Tarleton (Tavington in the film)—

were so personally insulted by the Swamp Fox and his victories. In their minds it was one thing to be defeated by a professionally trained army, yet quite another to be bested by "farmers with pitchforks," as the movie puts it. They thought Marion's tactics dishonorable, not becoming of a proper gentleman.

But here's what I want you to see: Marion didn't concern himself with his reputation among British officers. He cared only that his ragtag men and their guerrilla tactics would help defeat the occupying force and win the war.

JESUS'S RUGGED REPUTATION

Marion would have gotten along well with the Warrior Christ. After choosing his twelve-man squad, Jesus set out to accomplish the mission for which he was sent: preaching the good news to the poor, healing the sick, feeding the hungry, setting free the oppressed, and proclaiming that the time of the Lord's favor had come (Luke 4:18–19).

As you might imagine, this miracle-working prophet was a polarizing figure (John 7:43). Some thought he was the Rescuer sent from God and wanted to know more. Others doubted that this common man could be their long-awaited, God-sent Leader. But there was a third group—religious leaders who, jealous of his fame, sought to soil his reputation.

This is important to us because it shows that the Warrior Christ was a lot like us.

- He lived on the edge.
- He broke social norms.
- He made enemies.

If you've grown up with that sweet-faced Sunday-school Jesus, this may be news to you. But the Bible is clear. Jesus was not the prim and proper gentleman who always did what was expected of him and was loved by everyone. He was a wild-at-heart Ranger on a mission. He had calluses on his hands and dirt under his nails—rugged enough that tough fishermen wanted to drop everything to follow him.

If you are *not* a Christian, then I want you to meet this Jesus so that you can know he was not the religious stick-in-the-mud he is sometimes made out to be. He was truly a man's man. As a rural laborer, he knew how to work hard, and after quitting time, he knew how to play hard. He was "one of us." You need to know this Jesus so that you might join him on the Great Raid. After all, isn't this the kind of down-to-earth Leader you'd follow willingly?

> Jesus was not the prim and proper gentleman who always did what was expected of him and was loved by everyone. He was a wild-at-heart Ranger on a mission. ★

If you *are* a Christian, then I want you to know this Jesus so that you can become more like him. You can engage the secular world, as he did, and not run from it. We must stop thinking of our churches as fortresses, built to protect holy occupants from evil beyond the walls. Instead, we need to see churches as forward operating bases (FOBs)—temporary havens in a hostile place where recruits can train and veterans can heal, always with the intent of going back outside the wire! Isn't this what Jesus modeled for us? Wasn't this the very reason he came (Mark 1:38)?

Of course, being unconventional and surprising comes with a price.

THE EXPOSED FLANKS OF THE GREAT RAID

I want to show you what we can learn from how Jesus faced criticism, judgment, and derision from those stuck in the status quo. Why? Because there's just no way to fully follow the Warrior Christ without facing attacks from others along the way.

1. Jesus was attacked for his hometown.

Jerusalem was widely viewed as the center of religious life in Israel. A religious leader of any significance would surely make Jerusalem his home, most people thought. Seventy-five miles to the north, and in stark contrast to the Holy City, were the villages of Galilee—Jesus's home turf. To the city dwellers of Jerusalem, Galilee was "the sticks," full of country bumpkins who couldn't possibly know anything of God's laws (John 7:41, 49). The two regions were so distinct that a Galilean accent was easily recognized by Jews in Jerusalem (Matthew 26:73). Compare that with how the Manhattan elite might feel about the hillbillies of West Virginia, or what a Hollywood star might think about a cowboy from Amarillo.

When one Jewish leader tried to defend Jesus, others responded venomously, "Are you from Galilee, too? Search the Scriptures and see for yourself—no prophet ever comes from Galilee!" (John 7:52).

Even some of his followers had doubts. When Nathanael, a close associate of some recruits, first heard about Jesus and where he was from, he scoffed, "Nazareth! Can anything good come from Nazareth?" (John 1:46).

But what his enemies intended as an insult proved to be an asset in Jesus's mission. While his humble beginnings didn't draw attention from the spiritual elite, they were not necessarily his target audience. Remember the OPORD? He came to "bring Good News to the *poor*" (Luke 4:18). And he did that by coming as one of them—a carpenter's kid who probably played barefoot in the streets and caught crickets with other kids (Matthew 13:55). In fact, Jesus's reputation as a country boy, complete with the regional accent, only endeared him to his followers.

> Jesus is the kind of guy you sit next to on a bus and, before you know it, you've told him your whole life story. ★

We can relate to this kind of man. He's one of us. He's not a slick big-city politician or a polished megachurch preacher. He's the kind of guy you sit next to on a bus and, before you know it, you've told him your whole life story. Jesus turned his humble origins to his advantage, and so can we. Why? Because people struggling for hope all around us today know they can trust an everyday Joe.

2. Jesus was attacked for his behavior.

The second round of personal attacks that Jesus received was about the way he lived—specifically, his eating and drinking habits. Compared to John the Baptist, who lived in the desert, eating bugs and wild honey (Mark 1:6), Jesus loved to party. I'm serious! In fact, he acquired a reputation as "a glutton and a drunkard" (Matthew 11:19; Luke 7:34).

While this smear campaign embellished the truth, Jesus definitely understood the importance of good food and drink. Once he was at a week-long wedding party when the booze ran out. Rather than let the host lose face, Jesus (albeit reluctantly) kept the party going by turning ordinary water into around 150 gallons (equivalent to 750 bottles) of exceptional wine (John 2:1–11).

Some will argue that Jesus himself didn't drink, opting instead for the teetotaler image. I agree that Jesus was never intoxicated, as that is prohibited in Scripture (Ephesians 5:18). But it seems unlikely that he would have developed a reputation as a drunk (a clear exaggeration) if he never enjoyed a little wine now and then. Jesus even admitted that while his cousin John "[ate] no bread and [drank] no wine," he came both "eating and drinking" (Luke 7:33–34, NASB). Also, during his last meal with his recruits, Jesus said, "Mark my words—I will not drink wine *again* until the day I drink it new with you in my Father's Kingdom" (Matthew 26:29). Jesus certainly enjoyed a good drink here on earth, and by the sound of it, he is probably enjoying a great vintage with his Ranger buddies in heaven right now![2]

Jesus also enjoyed great food. When he invited Matthew and James to join his Ranger squad, Jesus was the guest of honor at a large banquet with his new recruits (Luke 5:29). I'm certain that the cuisine served at this wealthy home was exceptional. Later we see Jesus as an open-pit grill master. As his Rangers came in off the lake, Jesus was busy cooking an early meal of fish and bread over hot coals for himself and his friends (John 21:9). Calling out to these hungry fishermen, he said, "Now come and have some breakfast!" and he served them what he had prepared (vv. 12–13).

> Jesus didn't come to bring a "dry crust of bread" kind of religion but rather a "cup runneth over" kind of life. ★

His enemies intended the slur of "a glutton and a drunkard" to damage his reputation. In their eyes, a real prophet would abstain from eating and put on a sour demeanor to convey just how "holy" he was (Matthew 6:16). But Jesus blew that theory out of the water. He showed that the Kingdom of God is a realm filled with joy.

Every Ranger could tell you of times when the mission's urgency took priority over enjoying a meal. And sometimes, as crowds gathered around him, Jesus skipped eating, rather than miss an opportunity to fulfill his Commander's intent (Mark 3:20; 6:31). He even said, "My food is to do the will of him who sent me and to finish his work" (John 4:34, NIV). Jesus never put his personal enjoyment ahead of his Commander's objectives. There is no doubt that Jesus focused on his mission—but at the same time he modeled that a life of service can also be a life of joy!

My Rangers don't mope and frown on their way to a target. They love what they do, and it shows. Jesus wants the same enthusiasm from his recruits as we carry out his mission. His abundant life shows us that he didn't come to bring a "dry crust of bread" kind of religion but rather a "cup runneth over" kind of life (Psalm 23:5, KJV)!

3. Jesus was attacked for his friends.

The religious leaders assumed that a true prophet would spend time with righteous, upstanding citizens—people like them! But Jesus had neither the time nor the stomach for religious showmanship. Like many Rangers, he cared so much about the mission that he detested their pretentious posturing and airs of superiority. They were posers in the worst sense of the word. No wonder the religious elite were appalled (and personally offended) to see who Jesus chose to be with instead. Common criminals. Religious rejects. The spiritually substandard. As a result, these image-conscious leaders gave Jesus the derogatory reputation as "a friend of tax collectors and other sinners" (Matthew 11:19; Luke 7:34).

We need to understand that Jesus's contemporaries hated tax men even more than we do today. They were traitors. Though Jewish, they worked for the Romans, the despised invaders and occupying power. Tax men were also thieves. They routinely gathered more than required and pocketed the excess (Luke 19:8). Jesus pointed to tax collectors to illustrate the very bottom of moral behavior, equating them with non-Jews, who didn't know or follow God's rules (Matthew 5:46–47).

And yet Jesus befriended several.

Remember, Jesus recruited a tax collector named Matthew to join his twelve-man Ranger squad. That night, Matthew threw a big party for Jesus and invited his similarly unscrupulous friends to attend. When the religious leaders looked in, they asked, "Why does he eat with such scum?" (Mark 2:16). Later, Jesus approached a wealthy, senior tax man named Zacchaeus, and invited himself over for a meal. Again, the onlookers grumbled, "He has gone to be the guest of a notorious sinner" (Luke 19:7).

In those days, eating a meal in someone's home was a public declaration that you accepted him. It was the ancient equivalent of announcing in a bar, "Get this friend of mine a drink!" Everyone around would rightly conclude that you were on good terms. No wonder the religious leaders were offended (Luke 15:2).

Another unsavory group that Jesus befriended was unchaste women. Please don't misunderstand—Jesus was no more participating in their promiscuity than he was abetting the tax collectors' thievery. But his willingness to even address such women damaged his reputation.

When he spoke to the woman at the well (who had five previous husbands and was living with a sixth man), his own Ranger recruits "were shocked to find him talking to a woman" (John 4:18, 27). Yet she rushed back into town to tell everyone that the man who spoke to her just might be God's promised Rescuer.

Similarly, when an immoral woman poured perfume on Jesus's feet—washing them with her tears and drying them with her hair—Jesus commended her and forgave her sins, to the astonishment of the religious elite (Luke 7:37–48).

Rescuing these people was his mission all along! At Matthew's dinner party, when the few religious people there gave Jesus a hard time about associating with criminals, he responded, "Healthy people don't need a doctor—sick people do. I have come to call not those who think they are righteous, but those who know they are sinners" (Mark 2:17; Luke 5:31–32). Simply, Jesus loved people who were hurting and wanted to be with those who acknowledged their need for him.

Are you seeing a pattern in Jesus's unorthodox approach to his mission? The biblical Jesus was a wild Rescuer who defied social norms to accomplish his mission. As a boy, I was taught about a meek and mild Jesus. But as a man, I know I must put childish ways behind me and press on toward the goal of knowing Jesus as he truly is.

He was never embarrassed about his upbringing.

He celebrated life and enjoyed great food and wine.

He hung out with authentic people and despised the hypocrisy of the elite.

In all, Jesus didn't concern himself with reputation. He concerned himself with people, especially those in need. He knew who he was and what he was on mission to accomplish, and he wasn't about to change—no matter who disapproved.

If you choose to follow the example that Jesus set, then you, too, will face the criticism of others. On the one hand, you may have people in society brand you a "Jesus freak" or a "Bible thumper." On the other hand, the pious pew-sitters may call you "a friend of sinners" and attack you for hanging out with the wrong kind of people. But don't let that stop you from following this unorthodox Teacher from Galilee. He set out to please his Commander and reach those in need, regardless of the insults and hardship. And so must we.

A CALL TO ARMS

I recently had the privilege of hosting the parents of Private First Class Christopher Horns—one of our fallen Rangers—when they visited 2nd Ranger Battalion. On their first night in town, I suggested that they grab a few tables at a local pizzeria and let Rangers stop by to visit when they were released from work. When I arrived, Chris's mom offered me a shot of Jägermeister in honor of her son—his favorite drink.

In military culture, to refuse a drink in a setting like that would be to injure both the memory of a warrior and the generosity of a Gold Star mother who has already suffered enough.[3] What should I have done? What would you do?

I did what I thought my Leader would have done. I wholeheartedly accepted.

Tragically, I think the Jesus of our Sunday-school lessons would have politely declined (and many a pastor will recommend the same). But I can't find that Jesus anywhere in my Bible! Every page I turn reveals a rugged Rescuer who spent his life defying established religious norms—and had the reputation to prove it. Jesus's Rangers should have the same willingness to risk their reputation in order to be real with real people. Sadly, though, that's often not the case.

In its more than eighty-year history, Alcoholics Anonymous (AA) has done amazing things for thousands of former addicts, my dad among them. Imagine that at the next AA international board meeting they enact a policy that prevents alcoholics from coming to local meetings. After all, their lives are quite "unpleasant" and it makes some of the long-time attenders feel "uncomfortable." Can you see the irony? AA meetings filled with people who supposedly have it all together? What would be the point? Yet this seems to be a prevailing attitude in many of our churches.

So, what would it look like for us to emulate the common-man reputation of Jesus in today's culture? For starters, if a group of Christian men want to play a sport together, they could bypass the church league and sign up in their community. Bowl with the smokers. Play softball with the drinkers. Shoot hoops with the foul-mouthed.

If you have a men's prayer breakfast, don't host it at your church fellowship hall. Arrange to have it at the VFW building and invite local veterans. Host it at a rescue mission and bless the overworked and underappreciated staff. Meet at the gym of an underprivileged school and turn it into a service project.

> What others think about us is not as important as whether we're really infiltrating the world with the good news. ★

If you see that your coworker or neighbor could use a friend, don't start by inviting him to church—that's your turf. Offer to do something in his environment. Go out and grab a few beers. Check out the new motorcycle shop in town. Watch the big game at his place. Take every opportunity to make contact with people who wouldn't be caught dead in church. That seemed to be Jesus's modus operandi.

If we are to be like our Ranger Leader, we must cast aside a misguided concern for our reputation, roll up our sleeves, and engage in the fight. What others think about us is not as important as whether we're really infiltrating the world with the good news.

——

The battle lines have been drawn. Some stand with Jesus and others oppose him. And this divine Rescuer isn't about to back down from a fight, as we'll see in the chapter to come.

After Action Review

★ What characteristics often make a rural blue-collar worker more trustworthy than a polished city slicker? Why might it be important to people that Jesus came as a hardscrabble country boy?

★ Many of us were told—implicitly, if not overtly—that Jesus did not drink alcohol. If Jesus did imbibe, as Scripture suggests, how might that change the way you think of him?

★ What would it be like to sit beside Jesus at Matthew's banquet? Was he the life of the party or a religious killjoy? With regard to food and wine, what do you think was the balance that Jesus maintained? How should we behave in similar settings?

★ As a well-known Teacher, Jesus befriended unsavory people, stunning many who watched. Who are the "sinners" Jesus would likely hang out with today? And who would be shocked at it? What does this reveal about his heart and his mission for us?

★ Who are the "sick people" in need of a spiritual physician in your life or greater community? How can you better mirror this Ranger's engagement with the world—both in approach and in attitude?

CHAPTER 7

Confrontation

Standing Up for What's Right

Energetically will I meet the enemies of my country.

— from the fifth stanza of the Ranger Creed

If the world hates you, remember that it hated me first.

— John 15:18

My first chaplain assistant needed more help than I could give. Brian was a new soldier, a private fresh from basic training. So I attributed his late arrivals and incomplete tasks to immaturity. *He'll grow out of it,* I thought. Then something happened which revealed that the problem went deeper.

My wife and I hosted a weekend marriage retreat in Charlotte, North Carolina, three hours west of Fort Bragg. I met Brian at the battalion area Friday morning to help load equipment into the fifteen-passenger government van that he would be driving while I took my family in our car. I expected Brian to beat me to Charlotte, since he left a full hour earlier.

But driving down a remote highway, I saw a fifteen-passenger van approaching quickly from behind. While common on military bases, this vehicle was atypical for this part of the state. As it flew past me at well over the speed limit (problem 1), I saw Brian in the driver's seat talking on his cell phone (problem 2) and a young woman in the passenger seat (problem 3)! Not only had I directly told him that he could not bring a girl, but civilians are not allowed in government vehicles without authorization.

When I arrived at the retreat location, Brian and the van were nowhere in sight (problem 4)!

He finally showed up and spun a web of lies about where he had been and why he was late. Then I sprung the truth on him, and his story crumbled faster than a stale MRE cracker. Later, I wondered if my assertive tactic was the most Christian thing to do. How would Jesus have responded toward this blatant sin and irresponsibility? How should we? Maybe you've been in similar situations and wondered also.

It's time to change the perception that Jesus was a big softy. The truth is, he was willing to face off against evil and stand his ground. As his followers, so should we.

THREE RULES OF ENGAGEMENT

The common picture of Jesus looks a lot like Mister Rogers—kind, gentle, and compassionate. But the Gospels show Jesus being strong and aggressive when needed. A true Warrior, he stood his ground when provoked. Jesus modeled a mature masculinity—a controlled aggression—that can change how we see ourselves and how we respond to conflict.

As part of the Ranger Creed, each man swears to "energetically . . . meet the enemies of [his] country" and "defeat them on the field of battle." They do this by following the three rules of target engagement: acquire, identify, and engage.

> The common picture of Jesus looks a lot like Mister Rogers — kind, gentle, and compassionate. But the Gospels show Jesus being strong and aggressive when needed. ★

Here's what those rules mean:

- *A Ranger acquires a potential target.* He might see a person, silhouette, or shadow. He might hear a motorcycle or see vehicle lights moving in his direction. Any of these may threaten the strike force and as such is a potential target.

- *A Ranger identifies the target as hostile or friendly.* He is trained to look for weapons or other signs of nefarious intent. In night operations, he will quickly determine if the shape in front of him belongs to friend or foe.

- *A Ranger employs a weapon system to destroy a hostile target.* He might use his rifle or hand grenade. He might engage with machine gun or close air support. By whatever means, he will do everything in his power to protect his fellow Rangers and accomplish the mission.

These principles apply both to the individual Ranger and to the Ranger Task Force as a whole. Self-imposed constraints such as the three rules of target engagement separate honorable warriors from their unscrupulous opponents. Controlled aggression is what makes the Ranger regiment such a valuable asset and such a formidable foe.

These principles also fit followers of the Warrior Christ. Does that sound shocking? Let's look closer.

How to Fight Like the Warrior Christ

In the previous chapter, we saw how Jesus's controversial behavior earned him a negative reputation with the religious elite. Now we'll see how his provocative actions set him up for conflict with enemies of the truth. How did he handle that? What does it look like for you and me to fight like he did? That's what I want to show you in this chapter.

Jesus didn't bow to his enemies; he confronted them. The same principle holds true for us. When we encounter evil, it's okay—even Christlike—to confront that evil. We don't need to just be nice guys and hope it all goes away. The Warrior Christ gives us a model for handling ourselves during confrontations.

1. Jesus stayed on mission.

The first confrontation happened just after Jesus read the Commander's OPORD at the First Synagogue of Nazareth. In chapter 4, we concluded with Jesus sitting down and saying, "The Scripture you've just heard has been fulfilled this very day!" (Luke 4:21). But that is not where the story ends.

Now, the passage that Jesus read clearly referred to the coming Rescuer from God, who would save all humanity. The people knew this and, after hearing what Jesus said, began to murmur among themselves: "How can this be? Isn't this Joseph's son?" (v. 22).

Sensing their doubt, Jesus responded, "No prophet is accepted in his own hometown" (v. 24). The people wanted proof, but he refused. That sent the crowd into a rage. They jumped up, mobbed him, and forced him to the edge of a hill on which the town was built, ready to push him over the cliff (vv. 28–29).

What would you do in that situation? Maybe you'd run. Maybe you'd fight. The Bible says Jesus "passed right through the crowd and went on his way" (v. 30).

> When we encounter evil, it's okay—even Christlike—to confront that evil. We don't need to just be nice guys and hope it all goes away. ★

Wow! What just happened? Maybe this was some divine magic trick where Jesus somehow couldn't be touched. But I don't think so. We don't see such a tactic anywhere else in his mission.

Personally, I think Jesus gave them that Dirty Harry look that said, "Go ahead. Make my day." With sheer force of character, Jesus gave them a glare that said through clenched teeth, "I have a job to do. Get . . . out . . . of . . . my . . . way!" When they saw his determination, they lost their nerve, stepped aside, and let him pass.

He didn't fight. He didn't run. He simply went on his way. He didn't let anyone distract him from his mission. That's a great lesson for you and me.

Jesus didn't show fear but displayed incredible strength. Even when his life was threatened, he kept focused on his mission. A Ranger on a raid behind enemy lines does not compromise his position by engaging a roving patrol (a mobile security detachment), no matter how badly he wants to fight. He restrains himself and waits so he can fulfill the Commander's intent.

While at Ranger School, I conducted a reconnaissance mission for an upcoming raid. My element skillfully bypassed a three-man enemy lookout team so that we could observe the target compound undetected. Why destroy a fire team when you can take out the whole company? That's exactly what Jesus did. He avoided a skirmish . . . to prepare for war!

2. Jesus fought for the right reason.

Have you ever gotten burning mad when you saw some kind of injustice? I have. Jesus did too.

In his final week, Jesus traveled to Jerusalem. Approaching the temple grounds, Jesus did what any good Ranger would do before a mission: reconnaissance. "Jesus came to Jerusalem and went into the Temple. *After looking around carefully at everything,* he left because it was late in the afternoon" (Mark 11:11).

What did Jesus find on his initial recon? "In the Temple area he saw merchants selling cattle, sheep, and doves for sacrifices; he also saw dealers at tables exchanging foreign money" (John 2:14).

> You can't spell *Ranger* without the word *anger.* ★

Jewish law required that animals sacrificed at the temple be flawless. Some Jews didn't have a qualifying animal, and others traveled too far to bring along their own. So an industry sprang up where potential worshipers could buy unblemished animals on-site.

The industry itself was not the problem; it was the vendor dishonesty. The religious leaders did not permit foreign money in the temple, so people had to visit money-changers to get temple currency at an outrageous exchange rate. Then the people bought certified animals at inflated prices. They were being robbed twice just to obey God in worship!

That was too much for Jesus to take—religious leaders stealing from the very people they were charged to protect enraged him. I picture Jesus stewing on it all night as he calculated his response. In the morning, he let them have it.

> Jesus made a whip from some ropes and chased them all out
> of the Temple. He drove out the sheep and cattle, scattered
> the money changers' coins over the floor, and turned over
> their tables. Then, going over to the people who sold doves,
> he told them, "Get these things out of here. Stop turning my
> Father's house into a marketplace!" (John 2:15–16)

Just as he did during his duel with Satan, Jesus cited specific Old Testament passages to explain his anger. Addressing their dishonest abuse of power, Jesus shouted, "The Scriptures declare, 'My Temple will be called a house of prayer,' but you have turned it into a den of thieves!" (Matthew 21:13, from Isaiah 56:7 and Jeremiah 7:11).

Notice, you can't spell *Ranger* without the word *anger*. There is a place in our world for anger. But there's a difference between righteous anger and unrighteous anger. While we might get upset for selfish reasons—the driver ahead of us isn't going as fast as we want, or the store doesn't have the item we want, or our loved ones won't do what we want—Jesus got upset for the right reason. He saw clear injustice and could not stomach it! Jesus didn't just come to save us from personal sin, but, like a Ranger liberating an oppressed country, he came to rescue us from the sinful systems of this world.

3. Jesus countered with wisdom and truth.

An enemy's defenses get stronger as you get closer to the objective. So it's no surprise Jesus's opponents became fiercer as he approached the culmination of the Great Raid. The leaders—egos still bruised from Jesus's tirade in the temple—decided to set traps. They hoped Christ would either mishandle a religious question and lose his followers' loyalty or step into a political snare that would justify his arrest and execution (Matthew 22:15).

The first question was politically charged. "Now tell us what you think about this: Is it right to pay taxes to Caesar or not?" (v. 17).

Jesus saw right through the trap. If he said yes, he would lose the people's support, for many opposed Roman rule. If he said no, he would be branded a political zealot and executed for disturbing the peace.

But Jesus evaded the ambush. He noted the emperor's face was on the currency and told his questioners to "give to Caesar what belongs to Caesar, and give to God what belongs to God" (v. 21).

The next two traps had strong religious overtones. At that time, the two main groups of Jewish leaders had differing beliefs and thought they could divide Jesus's followers based on his answers.

One group asked, if a woman's husband dies and she remarries, and this happens seven times, whose wife will she be in the future resurrection (vv. 24–28)? (This group didn't believe in resurrection and thought that they could prove their case with this riddle.)

In response, Jesus—always a lightning rod for conflict—first insulted his opponents. "You are in error," he answered, "because you do not know the Scriptures or the power of God" (v. 29, NIV). *Ouch!* Then he silenced his critics, saying, "For when the dead rise, they will neither marry nor be given in marriage" and cited the Old Testament (vv. 30–32). This answer avoided the trap while affirming the future resurrection.

The second religious group took their turn: "Teacher, which is the most important commandment in the law of Moses?" (v. 36). (This law-focused group thought that by making him choose one they could show that he devalued the other commandments.) Again, Jesus evaded their trap:

> "You must love the LORD your God with all your heart, all
> your soul, and all your mind." This is the first and greatest
> commandment. A second is equally important: "Love your
> neighbor as yourself." The entire law and all the demands
> of the prophets are based on these two commandments.
> (vv. 37–40, from Deuteronomy 6:5 and Leviticus 19:18)

A great answer to a difficult question! Like a Ranger doing combatives training, Jesus had the opponent on his heels and moved in for the choke hold. Seizing the initiative, he went on the offensive with a question of his own:

> "What do you think about the [Rescuer]? Whose son is he?"
> They replied, "He is the son of David." (v. 42)

I can almost hear the religious leaders' mocking tone. "Really? That's your question? Any ten-year-old knows that! We have all read God's promise to David that the Rescuer would come from his descendants. Is that the best you've got?"

But they don't realize that Jesus had set a trap of his own.

Jesus responded, "Then why does David . . . call the [Rescuer] 'my Lord'? For David said,

'The LORD [God] said to my Lord [the Rescuer],
Sit in the place of honor at my right hand
    until I humble your enemies beneath your feet.'

Since David called the [Rescuer] 'my Lord,' how can the [Rescuer] be his son?" (Matthew 22:43–45, from Psalm 110:1)

Game. Set. Match. Jesus had handled with ease his opponents' three best serves. Then he fired a shot that shut them up. "After that," the Bible says, "no one dared to ask him any more questions" (v. 46).

The Jewish leaders might have been through with Jesus, but he was just getting warmed up. Turning to his Rangers and the crowd who had watched this battle of wits, he said:

The teachers of religious law . . . are the official interpreters of the law of Moses. So practice and obey whatever they tell you, but don't follow their example. For they don't practice what they teach. . . .
    Everything they do is for show. (Matthew 23:2–3, 5)

This salvo told the people that their religious leaders were spiritual frauds. But he wasn't finished. Six times, borrowing the Greek word for a stage actor, Jesus dubbed them "hypocrites." He meant that the leaders had put on masks of piety but underneath were wicked men. Five times, he called them "blind" and, specifically, "blind guides." He even called them murderers and the sons of murderers for their role in torturing and killing God's prophets (Matthew 23:13, 15–17, 19, 23–27, 29–34).

Clearly, Jesus was not just a gentle guru handing out flowers but a bold revolutionary and threat to those in power. I've shown you three situations that demonstrate how Jesus handled his attackers:

- His strength toward the lynch mob
- His violence toward the money-changers
- His boldness toward the fraudulent teachers

He faced his enemies and spoke his mind. He didn't apologize for offending. He didn't sugarcoat. His approach was direct and his message divisive.

> Jesus was not just a gentle guru handing out flowers but a bold revolutionary and threat to those in power. ★

A true Warrior, Jesus stated, "Do not think that I came to bring peace on the earth; I did not come to bring peace, but a sword" (Matthew 10:34, NASB). Like an invading general, he said, "I have come to bring fire on the earth, and how I wish it were already kindled!" (Luke 12:49, NIV). These are not the words of a pacifist. Jesus was the bellicose Ranger from God who came first and foremost to set things right, fully knowing the strife that his mission would require.

GOSPEL ARMY

When I reread these stories of Jesus, I feel like I am back in childhood reading comic books. I find myself cheering for the Hero to defeat the villain and save the day. But there's another reason I like these stories—I can relate to this Jesus more than the one I heard about in Sunday school. Knowing that Jesus was not afraid to fight gives me permission to fight for what's right too.

The Incarnation an invasion? The disciples as Ranger recruits? Some may not like these pictures. But it is hard to read these scriptures and not see Jesus as a consummate Warrior. Using the three rules of target engagement, he

- acquired a potential threat (religious leaders),
- identified the threat as hostile (thieves and hypocrites), and
- engaged the threat (flipped tables and verbally berated).

Rather than turn a blind eye to injustice, this Rescuer moved swiftly toward conflict and turned the tide of the battle.

> Knowing that Jesus was not afraid to fight gives me permission to fight for what's right too. ★

We are called to do the same. For this reason, one of my heroes is Dave Eubanks.

Dave grew up in Thailand as a missionary kid who dreamed of becoming a soldier. He realized this dream, serving for ten years as an Airborne Ranger and then a Special Forces officer. He understood what it meant to "close with and destroy the enemy." But God had something else in mind for this warrior.

In 1993, Dave received a phone call that changed his life. His father (still in Thailand) had met with some tribal leaders from Burma. They said, "We are a warrior people who need God. Your son is a warrior who follows God. Our people will listen to him. Please ask him to come."

For sixty years, the people of Burma have suffered under a brutal military dictatorship. Villages who resist are destroyed and the people murdered. But God did not forget the Burmese people. He sent Dave—a Christian warrior—to confront the evil in this foreign land.

In 1997, he founded a group called the Free Burma Rangers that trains native Burmese to move undetected through the hillsides to care for the people and preach the gospel. Today, they have seventy-five ethnic teams giving help, hope, and love in the conflict areas of Burma.

Their primary weapon against this murderous regime is not a rifle but prayer. Dave told me, "We confront evil by prayer and asking Jesus what to do. We have prayed in Jesus's name against demons that were manifested and seen people delivered. We have seen the Burma army turn back after prayer, and we have seen doors opened that were closed."

A Call to Arms

What Dave Eubanks has recognized—and what each of us needs to realize too—is that our world is at war. A spiritual war. Another leader embroiled in accusations of wrongdoing. Another family broken by infidelity. Another community ripped apart by hatred and distrust. The Enemy, like a skilled sniper, is picking us off one by one—our friends, our neighbors, even our own families. We can't hide in bunkers any longer. We need to follow the Warrior Christ and engage in the fight.

But how? I propose three important objectives that can give direction to your day:

1. We must win our personal battles.

Just as Jesus faced off against the Enemy in the desert, so we also face daily temptation. Satan, an expert deceiver, tries to convince us that we would be better off following his way than God's way.

- Should I remain faithful to my marriage vows? Satan whispers, "Don't you have a right to be happy?"
- Should I be completely honest in business practices? Satan suggests, "You'll lose the competitive edge!"
- Should I give up this secret pleasure? Satan hints, "But it's not hurting anyone!"

If we let his answers shape our thinking, we will be snared.

That is why Paul instructs us to "put on all of God's armor so that [we] will be able to stand firm against all the strategies of the devil" (Ephesians 6:11). If we get taken down in our personal battles, then how can we fight for others? If we don't win our one-on-one match-ups, we'll be useless in the larger battle.

2. We must fight for our families.

Your family is under attack. The Enemy would love to take you down, but he will settle for your loved ones if you are not on your guard.

Let me share a personal experience:

One night when my family and I were living at Fort Bragg, our one-year-old woke up with terrifying screams. My wife and I tried to console him in his crib. When that failed, we brought him into our room so he wouldn't wake his brother. Realizing that he was not yet awake, we took him into our bathroom, turned on the light, and splashed water on his forehead and cheeks. Still out cold, he continued to scream. After ten long minutes of night terrors, my wife, Bree, suggested that I pray. Foolishly, I tried to quiet my little one so I could begin. Bree told me to just pray over the commotion. All I got out was the word "Jesus" and my son stopped screaming and calmed down.

My experience is not the exception. The spiritual attack on my son that night was blatant. The Enemy, though, also has subtle schemes. Perhaps he starts with marital discord, creating a rift within the "command team" in the home. With our attention diverted, he picks off the most vulnerable—our kids. His tactic might be a temptation to experiment with a new substance or disregard healthy sexual boundaries. It might be an overwhelming sense of isolation and depression, leading to suicidal thoughts, or an outright rebellion against God and all earthly authority. Suddenly, the Enemy breaks through the perimeter and wreaks havoc within our ranks.

You are the guardian of your home. You are the gatekeeper against the spiritual forces that seek to steal, kill, and destroy (John 10:10). When Nehemiah was rebuilding defensive walls around Jerusalem, he placed men in the exposed gaps with their loved ones, telling them "to stand guard by families, armed with swords, spears, and bows" (Nehemiah 4:13).

You too have been called to stand in the gap and defend those you love. Don't fall asleep at your post!

3. We must fight for our community and the world.

If you're winning your personal battles and successfully defending your family, then it is time to go on the offensive. The truth is, Rangers are never really on the defensive. When it looks that way, they are merely reorganizing for counterattack. Defensive strategies, alone, are doomed to failure. Ask the Germans entrenched at Normandy, or the Japanese garrisoned at Cabanatuan. The offense always has the advantage because they choose the battle and fight on their terms.

Our world badly needs warriors for the downtrodden. God has charged us,

Help the oppressed.
    Defend the cause of orphans.
    Fight for the rights of widows. (Isaiah 1:17)

This may mean your personal involvement, squaring off against the oppressor for those less fortunate. This may require your personal resources, giving so that others might be saved from poverty, sickness, and death. Some head overseas to care for the impoverished. Others adopt orphans from war-torn nations. Some lead food or clothing drives to help nearby families in need. Others volunteer at their local school or homeless shelter. When I was growing up, my parents once took in a homeless Marine whom my dad met through AA until he could get back on his feet.

For several years, my family has participated in Advent Conspiracy. It is a program our church supports with the goal to spend less and give more over the Christmas season. We try to give relational gifts rather than retail gifts. Instead of scouring the mall, we make a date-night basket for each other or a photo scrapbook for the family. With the money we would have spent on presents, we let our kids "shop" on the World Vision website, buying small farm animals or clean water for children around the globe.

The ways you can engage in this fight are unlimited. If you are looking for it, God will show you the need and give you the heart to meet it.

So, where do we go from here?

Into the fight.

There are no sidelines in this battle. You must fight like Jesus did. You have been dropped into enemy territory for a mission. And your family, community, and world are counting on you. We have our marching orders. Let's move out!

———

Jesus threw down the gauntlet. He spit in the eye of the religious establishment. And then, with his enemies breathing death threats, he marched fearlessly into Jerusalem to complete his mission.

After Action Review

★ What do you think of the statement "The common picture of Jesus looks a lot like Mister Rogers"? Why do you think the church often prefers the mild Jesus over the real thing? How has this contributed to the absence and/or apathy of men in the church?

★ Jesus evaded a murder attempt at the synagogue in Nazareth. What can you conclude about him from this event? Was he a warrior or a pacifist? Did he show strength or fear? What would you have done?

★ Mark 11:11 suggests that Jesus had a night to prepare for his temple raid. How does that change your view of the event? Did he overturn tables in a fit of rage, a calculated attack, or both? Were his actions more consistent with a religious teacher or a seasoned soldier? Why?

★ On at least two occasions, Jesus intentionally antagonized religious leaders (Matthew 23; John 8). What does it say about Jesus and his mission that he directly challenged those who abused their authority? If Jesus picked a fight, then what might that mean for his followers today?

★ Jesus the Combatant calls us to join him in the fight. How are you doing in your personal battles? In your defense of your family? In your engagement with injustice in your community and the world? What will you do differently to fight and win in these three areas?

CHAPTER 8

Dedication

Finishing Your Mission, No Matter What

I volunteered as a Ranger, fully knowing the hazards
of my chosen profession.

— from the first stanza of the Ranger Creed

We're going up to Jerusalem, where the Son of Man
will be betrayed to the leading priests and teachers of
religious law. They will sentence him to die.

— Mark 10:33

J umpmaster, are you ready?"

When I turned around, I would face the first of three paratroopers, completely rigged and ready to jump. My task, as a student at
Advanced Airborne (a.k.a. Jumpmaster) School, was to thoroughly
inspect three jumpers in under five minutes and identify three pre-
arranged flaws in each parachute: two minor deficiencies (likely to
cause injury) and one major deficiency (likely to cause death). If I
missed a minor one, then I might be forgiven. If I missed a major

deficiency, then I'd fail the exam. I had already tested twice—unsuccessfully.

This was my third and final attempt.

With a deep breath and a short prayer, I spun around as the stopwatch chirped. My hands flew over various parachute components. I tapped on canopy release assemblies and traced the yellow static line, my eyes never more than six inches away.

My first jumper went well. I found the major and the two minors and firmly tapped the jumper on the hip to tell him (and the instructor peering over my shoulder) that I had completed my inspection and the parachute was safe.

The second inspection, same.

But as I reached the end of my third inspection sequence, I had not found the major deficiency. I panicked. Had I missed it?

With time running out and no way to reinspect, I tapped the jumper on the hip and awaited the outcome. As soon as I had given the "seal of approval," there was no going back. Tactically speaking, it was the line of departure (LD); the point of no return. Either I would graduate as a jumpmaster or I'd return to my unit with the ignoble label "no-go"—Army jargon for failure.

The instructor turned his stopwatch toward me: 4:47. I was good for time.

Then he ominously pointed at the reserve parachute of the third jumper. Was he indicating a major deficiency that I had failed to find? My fate rested at the end of his extended finger. "What do you see there?" he asked.

I saw no flaws and told him the same.

He gestured a second time and said, "Look again."

At this point I caught onto his game. "There's nothing there," I said.

He smiled. "You're a 'go,'" he said. "Congratulations!"

We've all encountered some sort of "line of departure" in our lives. A challenge faces us and we need the resolve to continue forward and cross the point of no return.

A line of departure can be as straightforward as hitting Send on an important e-mail. Or dropping a report on a boss's desk. Saying "I do" in marriage is a huge line of departure. So is adding a child to your family. In those events, there is no turning back. It takes courage to step across that line. The same kind of courage we see in the Warrior Christ.

> We've all encountered some sort of "line of departure" in our lives. A challenge faces us and we need the resolve to continue forward and cross the point of no return. ★

Jesus crossed his LD when he entered Jerusalem on a donkey the Sunday before his death. He knew exactly what awaited him, yet he went anyway. Do you have the dedication it takes to follow Jesus on the Great Raid beyond the point of no return, regardless of the cost? This chapter will help you identify—and cross—your own line of departure.

RANGERS LEAD THE WAY!

On the night of June 5, 1944, Lieutenant Colonel James E. Rudder, commander of 2nd Ranger Infantry Battalion, and his men boarded a transport ship bound for Normandy, France. They had been training for this mission for months and were ready to execute their assigned tasks. Rudder and D, E, and F companies of 2nd Rangers would climb the cliffs at Pointe du Hoc—a salient bluff between Omaha and Utah beaches—and silence the German cannons above. Meanwhile, 5th Ranger Infantry Battalion, with A, B, and C companies of 2nd Rangers, would land on Omaha Beach. This Ranger unit and their amphibious assault are vividly depicted in the opening scenes of Steven Spielberg's war epic *Saving Private Ryan*.

In the fall of 2012, I got to meet one of the veterans who stormed the beaches with the 5th Rangers. He sought me out after a ceremony to tell me about Father Joe Lacy, his chaplain on D-day. The night before the invasion, Father Lacy brought the battalion together and told them, "When you get on the beaches, I don't want to see any of you praying. If you do, I'm gonna come up there and boot you in the tail. You do the fighting and leave the praying to me."

Father Lacy and his Rangers had been ready the night before, but the execution of Operation Overlord, the invasion of Normandy, had been delayed because of weather. As Rudder and his men sailed southeast toward France, they knew that somewhere in that vast English Channel was their line of departure—the point at which there would be no more delays and no turning back. Rudder and his men must have realized that they had reached the LD when, at 4:05 a.m. on June 6, the order came to board the LCAs (landing craft, assault). As they climbed down the netting into the boats below, they faced only two possible outcomes: victory or death.

D-day commanders at all levels understood that once they crossed the LD, their only chance of survival was to push beyond the deadly beach. On Omaha that day, Brigadier General Norman Cota, assistant commander of the 29th Infantry Division, was frustrated by the inaction of many men and the stalled attack. Finding some 5th Battalion Rangers, he implored them to set the example for the rest of the troops, calling out, "Rangers, lead the way!" That brief sentence, shouted over the din of machine gun and mortar fire, later became the unofficial motto of the U.S. Army Rangers.

For Colonel Rudder and the men of 2nd Battalion, the cliffs of Pointe du Hoc grew larger and larger as they approached in the landing craft. Towering one hundred feet above the water, the rock must have seemed insurmountable. Using grappling hooks and rope ladders, these Rangers scaled the cliffs while fighting off German defenders above. They had crossed the LD; there would be no withdrawal, no retreat. Their only choice was to go forward.

True to their reputation as Rangers, Rudder and his men did exactly what was needed. They pressed forward, eliminated the artillery battery, and completed the mission.[1]

Always Pressing On

Similar to the World War II Rangers, Jesus had no false notions about his mission and what it would cost. For three years, he had been preparing himself and his men for this final assault on the Enemy—the culmination of the Great Raid. At last the moment of decision had come. It was time for him to cross the LD.

The line of departure for Jesus was his entrance into Jerusalem on Sunday morning, five days before his death. Once through the city gates, there would be no turning back.

Earlier, Jesus had definitely grasped this fact. "As the time drew near for him to ascend to heaven," the Bible says, "Jesus *resolutely set out for Jerusalem*" (Luke 9:51). Later, we see the same strong drive to accomplish the mission. "Jesus went through the towns and villages, teaching as he went, *always pressing on toward Jerusalem*" (Luke 13:22). He understood that the decisive point in this fight would be the Holy City, and he was determined to get there. The fate of humanity hung in the balance.

> The line of departure for Jesus was his entrance into Jerusalem on Sunday morning, five days before his death. Once through the city gates, there would be no turning back. ★

In the months leading up to the LD, Jesus had been telling his men details of the mission ahead. His recruits needed to be mentally prepared. We sometimes call this type of briefing a warning order (WARNO), a formal "heads-up" that lets subordinates know that a mission is in the works. Although not as detailed as a full OPORD, it provides the plan's basic concept so that the Rangers can get ready for what lies ahead.

> From then on Jesus began to tell his [recruits] plainly that it was necessary for him to go to Jerusalem, and that he would suffer many terrible things at the hands of the elders, the leading priests, and the teachers of religious law. He would be killed, but on the third day he would be raised from the dead. (Matthew 16:21)

Peter got visibly upset at this, saying, "Heaven forbid, Lord. This will never happen to you!" (v. 22). Jesus firmly rebuked Peter, but the Ranger squad still didn't get the message. Twice more, on different occasions, Jesus restated the WARNO (Matthew 17:22–23; 20:17–19).

Finally, it seems, his Ranger squad understood why they must cross the LD. The Holy City was about to become a battlefield where humanity's greatest Warrior would close with and destroy the Enemy of our souls *and rescue us once and for all!*

ENTERING THE CITY

Jesus could have slipped through the city's gates under the cover of darkness and kept a low profile. He had done that before (John 7:10). But the occasion for stealth was over. Jesus would make a bold statement this time—one that both followers and foes would not soon forget.

For centuries, conquering armies had marched into walled cities with great fanfare. Often, defeated citizens were made to line the road as a commanding general or the emperor himself paraded through the streets atop a chariot or regal mount. Jesus borrowed some of this imagery during his entrance into Jerusalem—to the wonder of some and the disgust of others.

As this Ranger commander and his twelve recruits approached the Holy City, Jesus sent a two-man advance party to procure a mount for his Triumphal Entry. But unlike a conqueror, he didn't pick a fine white stallion. Instead, he borrowed a young donkey. He even promised to return the beast (Mark 11:2–3)! This was not the preferred mode of travel for a distinguished general or dignified monarch, but Jesus was implementing his Commander's instructions.

Rejoice, O people of Zion!
Shout in triumph, O people of Jerusalem!
Look, your king is coming to you.

He is righteous and victorious,
yet he is humble, riding on a donkey—
    riding on a donkey's colt. (Zechariah 9:9)

As if on cue, the people in Jerusalem responded like a victorious emperor was entering the city, only this worship was sincere. This King was not their conqueror but their Rescuer. The New Testament records the scene:

When they reached the [city], all of his followers began to
shout and sing as they walked along, praising God for all the
wonderful miracles they had seen. (Luke 19:37)

Most of the crowd spread their garments on the road ahead
of him, and others cut branches from the trees and spread
them on the road. Jesus was in the center of the procession,
and the people all around him were shouting,

    "Praise God for the Son of David!
    Blessings on the one who comes in the name of
        the LORD!
    Praise God in highest heaven!" (Matthew
        21:8–9)

    Praise God! . . .
    Blessings on the coming Kingdom of our
        ancestor David! (Mark 11:9–10)

What a spectacle! A poor country preacher arriving on a borrowed donkey seems fitting. But for crowds to treat him as the coming

King of Israel and promised Rescuer from David's family seems ludicrous. I doubt even Jesus's followers expected such a warm response.

> The Triumphal Entry was Jesus's last covered and concealed position. From here on, he was exposed and subject to the Enemy's firepower. ★

But not everyone celebrated. For the religious rulers, this parade was too much. When they insisted that he rebuke his followers, Jesus retorted, "If they kept quiet, the stones along the road would burst into cheers!" (Luke 19:40). If ever there was a victorious hero who knew how to make an entrance (and aggravate a few people in the process), it was Jesus.

Infantrymen speak of the "last covered and concealed position" before the assault. After this location, you are in full view of the enemy and subject to the full effects of their weapon systems. The Triumphal Entry was Jesus's last covered and concealed position. From here on—like the soldiers who stormed the beaches at Normandy—he was exposed and subject to the Enemy's firepower. But he faced the barrage without fear. In a few short days, he would give his life to save us all.

THE SIGNIFICANCE OF THE LAST MEAL

The Great Raid had entered its final hours. Jesus had crossed his line of departure when he entered Jerusalem. But for his followers, their LD still lay ahead. Would they continue the mission that he started? Or would they scatter "like sheep without a shepherd" (Matthew 9:36; 26:31)?

The consummate Leader, Jesus brought his twelve-man squad together for a final meal before they entered battle the next day. Like Rudder and his men on the eve of D-day, Jesus wanted to share last-minute instructions and celebrate one last time together. A Thursday night dinner that we know as the Last Supper provided Jesus with the perfect opportunity for three final messages to his troops.

1. A memorial event

This meal was actually a Passover celebration (Mark 14:14), a centuries-old Jewish holiday commemorating Moses's mission to rescue God's people from a foreign power. Just as the Fourth of July recalls American independence from Britain, so Passover recalls Israel's miraculous escape from slavery in Egypt.

Drawing on the parallel between Passover and his upcoming rescue mission, Jesus infused the holiday meal with new meaning. No longer would his followers remember what Moses did to liberate Israel, but what Jesus did to set all people free.

> When the time came, Jesus and [his recruits] sat down together at the table. . . .
>
> He took some bread and gave thanks to God for it. Then he broke it in pieces and gave it to the [recruits], saying, "This is my body, which is given for you. *Do this to remember me.*" (Luke 22:14, 19)

For more than a millennium, Jews had celebrated Passover to remember the most significant event in their history: God using Moses to lead their escape from captivity and oppression in a foreign land. Now one who deserves greater honor than Moses was there (Hebrews 3:3). The meal instituted by Jesus was to be a constant reminder of his Great Raid—the most anticipated and extraordinary event in human history.

In the U.S. military, we build memorials to remember major events in our histories. The Marine Corps War Memorial vividly depicts the flag raising on Mount Suribachi to honor the fallen at Iwo Jima and across the Pacific. The Navy's USS *Arizona* Memorial solemnly rests atop Pearl Harbor's underwater crypts and recalls the lives lost on that "day which shall live in infamy." For Army Rangers, no memorial is more hallowed than the inverted dagger atop the salient cliffs of Pointe du Hoc in Normandy. It harkens back to an elite group of men who did the impossible to liberate a continent. Just as these memorials honor those who died for freedom, so Jesus's memorial meal honors the divine Rescuer who died to set us free.

2. A leadership lesson

Jesus used this meal to teach his recruits how to carry on his mission after his death. He knew that they would be thrust into leadership in this fledgling new Ranger outfit called the church. Wanting them to lead with humility, in contrast to the political powers of the day, he said:

> You know that the rulers of this world lord it over their people, and officials flaunt their authority over those under them. But among you it will be different. Whoever wants to be a leader among you must be your servant, and whoever wants to be first among you must become your slave. For even the [Rescuer] came not to be served but to serve others and to give his life as a ransom for many. (Matthew 20:25–28)[2]

Jesus never asked his recruits to do anything he himself would not do. Both his life and his death were perfect examples of the selfless service we aspire to in the military. But to give his recruits a visual reminder, he demonstrated servant leadership in the most humbling way. Though a respected rabbi, he assumed the role of slave and washed his men's feet. Then he said:

> Do you understand what I was doing? You call me "Teacher" and "Lord," and you are right, because that's what I am. And since I, your Lord and Teacher, have washed your feet, you ought to wash each other's feet. I have given you an example to follow. Do as I have done to you. (John 13:12–15)

In that culture—with open shoes, dusty roads, and floor-level tables—foot washing was an important practice, both for hygiene and for courtesy. Jesus once chided his host, a religious ruler, for not providing water for his feet (Luke 7:44). Typically, the foot washer would be the lowest-ranking person available. In wealthier homes, this unpleasant duty was often delegated to a servant girl. But here, violating custom, the Leader became the Servant to set a pattern for his men. Jesus certainly exhibited the Ranger training philosophy of "lead by example."

3. A promotion ceremony

So far, we have referred to Jesus's twelve-man Ranger squad as "recruits." While clearly a military analogy, this is fairly accurate. A recruit is in a learning role. He must absorb both verbal instruction and physical demonstration of his cadre if he is to become a Ranger himself.

This is exactly the situation with Jesus's specially selected unit.

For three years, these men have spent almost every moment with their Teacher. They have listened to him teach, watched him perform miracles, and obeyed his every word. Finally, these twelve recruits were ready for promotion to full-fledged Rangers. Following the meal, Jesus gave the graduation address.

> This is my commandment: Love each other in the same way
> I have loved you. There is no greater love than to lay down
> one's life for one's friends. You are my friends if you do what
> I command. I no longer call you [recruits] because a [com-
> mander] doesn't confide in his [recruits]. Now you are my
> friends, since I have told you everything the Father told me.
> (John 15:12–15)

In the middle of this speech lies a sentence that resonates deep inside every soldier, no matter his or her faith. It has been read at many military funerals and inscribed on many war memorials: *"There is no greater love than to lay down one's life for one's friends."* In those simple words, Jesus captured something that many Rangers have felt. These battle-hardened men who often recoil at tenderness and laugh at affection will unequivocally and unabashedly state that they would give their lives for a Ranger buddy. Jesus certainly grasped—and would soon display—the heart of a warrior.

———

In his final hours, Jesus took time with his men to impart a new memorial, instruct a new teaching, and introduce a new relationship. His men were ready to be shipped out to battle.

REFUSING TO QUIT

Jesus showed great dedication in crossing his line of departure and getting to the objective. No one could distract or dissuade him from his mission, though many tried. In his march to the Holy City, he demonstrated the steely resolve and razor-sharp focus of a warrior, hellbent on getting to the target location. Could the same be said of us? Are we dedicated to follow our Leader onto the Ranger objective and complete the mission, regardless of the cost?

Ghassan Thomas, an ordinary Muslim young man growing up in Iraq under the rule of Saddam Hussein, encountered—and crossed—his line of departure. Ghassan had a cousin who told him about Jesus and prayed for him for ten years. Finally, in 1992, he found his way into a church and enlisted in God's mission. There was no turning back.

> When Ghassan put a sign outside his church that read "Jesus is the Light of the World," someone scrawled "Jesus is not the light of the world. Allah is, and you have been warned." ★

After studying theology in Lebanon, he returned to Iraq in 1999 and intended to start a church in Baghdad. The government threatened him. So he opened a school instead and held secret services in his home. They threatened him still. Ever faithful, he started to preach openly at his school. That was the final straw. Soldiers came to find and kill Ghassan, but—warned in advance—he fled to Syria.

Three weeks later, U.S. troops rolled into Iraq and answered

Ghassan's prayers to return to his home country. In April 2003, only weeks after the invasion, Pastor Thomas opened a church in Baghdad. Saddam may have been removed, but there were still threats from the Muslim community. When Ghassan put a sign outside his church that read "Jesus is the Light of the World," someone scrawled "Jesus is not the light of the world. Allah is, and you have been warned."

Despite the persecution, the church in Baghdad thrived, growing to over one thousand members. Ghassan clearly heard God's call and fearlessly followed him across the line of departure.

A CALL TO ARMS

If you, like Ghassan Thomas, are considering following the first and greatest Airborne Ranger into the fray, then you need to know the dangers. This is not a mission for the faint of heart. Look at the men who took up the cause after Jesus.

- Stephen was stoned to death (Acts 7:59–60).
- James was killed with a sword (Acts 12:2).
- John was banished to a small, rocky island (Revelation 1:9).
- Peter was jailed and flogged for his faith (Acts 4:3; 5:18, 40).
- Paul was beaten with rods, lashed with a whip, pummeled with stones, and left for dead (2 Corinthians 11:24–25).

In fact, if the history books are to be believed, every single one of the eleven faithful Rangers, except John, gave his life as a martyr for the cause of the Great Raid.

Despite all that, these men rejoiced because "God had counted them worthy to suffer disgrace for the name of Jesus" (Acts 5:41). These early Rangers followed a Warrior Christ across the line of departure and gladly suffered violence on his behalf.

As you fight your personal battles, you will face trials and hardship. As you defend your family from spiritual attack, you are bound to take a few blows. As you move out of the bunker and cross the LD on behalf of your community, you are sure to come under fire. This is the cost of doing battle—no one comes out unscathed. Still interested?

If you step across the LD by volunteering for a ministry in your church or community, there are bound to be difficulties. You may give up evenings or weekends. You may encounter people who are difficult to work with. But it is worth it to be involved in what God is doing in the world.

> Some would rather remain in cozy faith bunkers and wait for the war to be over. But a Ranger swiftly moves to the sound of the guns that he might bravely fight— and perhaps give his life—in the relentless pursuit of a noble cause. ★

If you cross an LD by adding a child to your family—whether by birth or adoption—there is no turning back. You will face long, sleepless nights. You will work tirelessly to provide for someone who may not even thank you. But it is worth it to watch her learn and grow into the person God made her to be.

If you go past the LD by committing to go overseas or across town to share the good news about Jesus, you are certain to encounter resistance. You may face harsh conditions as you venture outside of what is safe and comfortable. You may experience stiff resistance as people reject both you and your message. But it is worth it to see the joy on the face of someone who is hearing about the love of God for the first time.

Some will hear of the difficulties and shy away from the battlefield. They would rather remain in cozy faith bunkers and wait for the war to be over. But a Ranger swiftly moves to the sound of the guns that he might bravely fight—and perhaps give his life—in the relentless pursuit of a noble cause. Our world is full of danger and in desperate need of warriors. Fully knowing the hazards ahead, Jesus took up the mission and crossed the LD. And he calls us to do the same.

There is an old church chorus we sang when I was growing up. Its words accurately convey the dogged determination we need:

I have decided to follow Jesus.
I have decided to follow Jesus.
I have decided to follow Jesus.
No turning back, no turning back.

That simple refrain causes me to picture the Warrior Christ leaping out from a covered position and charging an enemy machine gun nest, bayonet fixed on the end of his rifle for the assault. I'm there behind cover as well—and so are you. In the heat of the moment, we jump to our feet and charge out beside our Leader. We will follow him come what may.

No turning back, no turning back.

———

As Jesus crossed the LD, he knew that the cross—his life's objective—lay ahead. Like a Ranger, he didn't hesitate but moved quickly to the target, the point of greatest danger.

After Action Review

★ The line of departure (LD) is the tactical point of no return. How was Jesus's entrance into Jerusalem an LD? What does it say about this Ranger that he was so determined to get to his objective?

★ How was the Triumphal Entry similar to the arrival of an invading general or conquering monarch? How was it different? What does this lowly mode of transportation say about its rider (Zechariah 9:9)? How was it consistent with his upbringing and ministry?

★ Jesus repurposed the Passover meal and infused it with new meaning. How was his rescue mission similar to the one carried out by Moses centuries earlier? How does the metaphor of a war memorial change your view of eucharist/communion? Can a memorial be both solemn and celebratory? Why or why not?

★ The recruits' promotion ceremony was preceded by an object lesson of their Leader becoming their Servant. What did the foot washing demonstrate to these Rangers about their upcoming mission? What does it say about the way we are to engage with others?

★ Jesus and his earliest followers were completely sold out for this mission. Why are we sometimes reluctant to go all in for this calling? What does it look like to cross the LD in your life?

CHAPTER 9

Crucifixion

Giving Your Life Away to Rescue Others

Readily will I display the intestinal fortitude required
to fight on to the Ranger objective and complete the
mission.

— from the sixth stanza of the Ranger Creed

There is no greater love than to lay down one's life for
one's friends.

— John 15:13

F all 1993. Members of 3rd Ranger Battalion were sent to Mogadishu, Somalia, as a part of Operation Gothic Serpent. Their
mission was to kill or capture Mohamed Farrah Aidid, a prominent
warlord and self-proclaimed president, and dismantle his militia,
who were stealing humanitarian aid sent to that impoverished
nation.

On October 3, a hundred-man Ranger company, with other
special operations personnel — dubbed Task Force Ranger —
conducted a daring afternoon raid aimed at two high-level

lieutenants near the city's hostile Bakara Market. During the operation, depicted so vividly in the movie *Black Hawk Down,* Aidid's militia crippled two U.S. helicopters, which crashed onto the streets below. The raid suddenly became a rescue and recovery mission.

> Randy Shughart and Gary Gordon valiantly defended their brother from dozens of armed assailants until both men fell to enemy gunfire. ★

Two special operations snipers, Sergeant First Class Randy Shughart and Master Sergeant Gary Gordon, could see the downed aircraft from their own helicopter, circling above the city. They knew that the aircrews inside would soon be swarmed by angry Somalis, so these brave men requested permission to land and defend one crash site. Commanders rightly saw this as a suicide mission and initially denied approval, but seeing the men's determination, they finally agreed.

Shughart and Gordon landed and pulled the sole crash survivor, Chief Warrant Officer Mike Durant, from the wreckage. They valiantly defended their brother from dozens of armed assailants until both men fell to enemy gunfire. Chief Durant was then captured by Aidid's militiamen.

Meanwhile, Rangers who had been on blocking positions around the raid building moved quickly to the other crash site. Simultaneously, a Ranger-led ground convoy of lightly armored vehicles made its way through the crowded and obstacle-laden streets to help. Both elements were under heavy fire and taking casualties. It soon became clear that this "one-hour mission" would last through the night. At first light, an armored convoy finally arrived to evacuate the besieged men of Task Force Ranger—the exhausted, the wounded, and the fallen.[1]

Eighteen American warriors—Rangers, air crewmen, and special operators—lost their lives on the streets of Mogadishu during the mission. Most fell after the helicopters went down. And so they didn't really die snatching enemy leaders but rescuing warrior brothers. These men understood and exemplified the Ranger Creed: "I will never leave a fallen comrade to fall into the hands of the enemy."

Eleven days later, Chief Durant was handed over to U.S. forces and returned safely home. He owed his life to the sacrifice of Shughart and Gordon. For their heroic and selfless deeds, both men were posthumously awarded the Medal of Honor. Like the divine Ranger, they gave their lives to save another.

The Warrior Christ exchanged his life for ours. In doing so, he modeled for us how to boldly give our lives away. We may not actually die through taking part in the Great Raid. (But then again, we might! After all, millions have.) Certainly we will have to give up much. Comfort, security, acceptance—all these things and more might have to go if we are to be faithful to God and his mission in this world.

There's a cost to pay in following the Rescuer. But it is so worth it.

Jesus said to his [recruits], "If any of you wants to be my follower, you must turn from your selfish ways, take up your cross, and follow me. If you try to hang on to your life, you will lose it. But if you give up your life for my sake, you will save it." (Matthew 16:24–25)

He showed us the way.

THE PRAYER

Jerusalem. The great city of David and the chosen dwelling place of God. The name means "a habitation of peace." And yet, for the divine Rescuer, it became a blood-soaked battlefield in the ancient war to defeat the Enemy and rescue humanity.

Every Ranger prepares himself for a mission a little differently. Some put in their earbuds and get amped up to angry music. Some are quiet, focusing on their role in the mission. Still others recite Psalm 91 or whisper a quick prayer as they put on their equipment and head to the vehicles.

Similarly, just hours before the final phase of the Great Raid started, Jesus spent time alone with his Commander to review the mission. He wanted to ensure that his head was in the right place. After his final meal with his Rangers, Jesus grabbed his squad and headed to an olive grove named Gethsemane (Mark 14:32).

Consistent with Ranger practice, Jesus put his men into a small security halt and gave them a clear task: "Pray that you will not give in to temptation" (Luke 22:40). Even though Jesus was about to enter the most difficult and dangerous phase of the operation, he didn't ask his subordinates to pray for him. Jesus was always concerned for the safety and success of his men.

Jesus then took Peter, James, and John and moved a stone's throw away. He gave these three—his finest Rangers—a specific task: "Stay here and keep watch with me" (Matthew 26:38). "Keep watch" means exactly what an infantry soldier thinks it means: stay awake, stay alert, and keep a sharp eye out for trouble! Aware of the danger they would face that night, Jesus appropriately put his men at 100 percent security.

Knowing that his men would be on overwatch, Jesus stepped away, bowed his head to the ground, and prayed,

> My [Commander]! If it is possible, let this cup of suffering
> be taken away from me. Yet I want your will to be done, not
> mine. (v. 39)

Jesus knew that the Great Raid would be costly. He knew that his blood would need to be spilled to accomplish the mission. Of course it was daunting for him, just as the costs of your own mission are going to be daunting to you sometimes. Fear and anxiety are sometimes reasonable reactions to what lies ahead. But our fears must not stop us, just as Jesus didn't let his fears stop him. He confirmed his Commander's intent and affirmed his own obedience.

Meanwhile, twice Jesus returned to his three-man element and found them all asleep. Both times, he woke his weary Rangers and encouraged them to continue praying. When he returned to sleeping soldiers a third time, frustrated by their fatigue, Jesus resorted to sarcasm (a favorite technique among drill sergeants and Ranger instructors). "Go ahead and sleep! Have your rest!" (v. 45, punctuation added).[2] But before he could say more, he was interrupted by the sound of footsteps and the flash of torches.

THE ARREST

Approaching their security halt in the olive grove was a military detachment of Roman soldiers and temple guards, the personal troops of the religious establishment in Jerusalem (John 18:3). Guiding the martial mob was a disgruntled Ranger turncoat—an insider threat—who had previously agreed to turn over Jesus for a handsome price (Matthew 26:15). Judas was familiar with Gethsemane and led the detachment straight to the Rescuer and his men (John 18:2). He betrayed Jesus with a kiss (Mark 14:44–45).

Many times, I have seen Rangers suddenly snap into focused and fearless action when the fighting starts. You might likewise find your God-given courage arise within you when the situation you've worried about finally arrives. That's what happened with Jesus.

> Like an excerpt from a Medal of Honor citation, Jesus displayed "utter disregard for his own safety" and showed "the utmost concern for the welfare of his men." ★

As the armed men closed in behind the betrayer, Jesus didn't cower or run. He didn't try to hide from his assailants. Like a fearless Ranger, he faced them head-on.

> Jesus fully realized all that was going to happen to him, so he stepped forward to meet them. "Who are you looking for?" he asked.
> "Jesus the Nazarene," they replied.
> "I AM he," Jesus said. . . . As Jesus said "I AM he," they all drew back and fell to the ground! (John 18:4–6)

The coalition of soldiers didn't expect this. They'd arrested many criminals and degenerates before. They'd seen men run and hide, deceive and squirm, or stand and fight. But they had never seen one demonstrate the strength of character required to step forward and willingly confess his identity. They were startled right off their feet!

As they dusted themselves off from their fall, Jesus resumed his aggressive, Rangerlike stance.

> Once more he asked them, "Who are you looking for?"
>
> And again they replied, "Jesus the Nazarene."
>
> "I told you that I AM he," Jesus said. "And since I am the one you want, let these others go." (vv. 7–8)

Jesus was more concerned with his men's safety than with his own. In those days, soldiers typically arrested everyone associated with a criminal and let the courts sort it out. Few were ever released but rather were declared guilty by association and executed along with their ringleader. Aware of this, Jesus willingly dove on the judicial hand grenade and offered his own life to spare his Rangers. Like an excerpt from a Medal of Honor citation, Jesus displayed "utter disregard for his own safety" and showed "the utmost concern for the welfare of his men." His heroism was already the stuff of legend, and this phase of the Great Raid had only begun.

But his men didn't stand idly by and let him get captured. Like good Rangers, they stepped up to fight. "When those who were around Him saw what was going to happen, they said, 'Lord, shall we strike with the sword?'" (Luke 22:49, NASB). One didn't wait for Jesus's response. Peter, the impulsive infantryman, was all too eager to draw blood.

> Simon Peter drew a sword and slashed off the right ear of
> Malchus, the high priest's slave. But Jesus said to Peter, "Put
> your sword back into its sheath. Shall I not drink from the

cup of suffering the [Commander] has given me?" (John 18:10–11)

While I respect Peter's zeal, I can't help but admire Jesus's restraint. The Warrior Christ certainly could have ordered his men to attack, but it wouldn't have been a fair fight. Fishermen and tax collectors against professional soldiers? They wouldn't have stood a chance. Jesus could have called for heavenly reinforcements, but that would have jeopardized his Commander's mission (Matthew 26:53). Jesus demonstrated further restraint and compassion by healing the ear that Peter had severed (Luke 22:51).

Turning to the soldiers and religious leaders, Jesus confronted their cowardice:

> Am I some dangerous revolutionary . . . that you come with
> swords and clubs to arrest me? Why didn't you arrest me in
> the Temple? I was there every day. But this is your moment,
> the time when the power of darkness reigns. (vv. 52–53)

Instead of a public arrest that might have incited a riot, these spineless bureaucrats opted for a night ambush, knowing that envy, not justice, motivated this attack. They bound him (John 18:12) and "began mocking and beating him" (Luke 22:63–65). Jesus was now a POW. His Rangers, meanwhile, had all deserted him and fled (Matthew 26:56).

THE TRIAL

Abandoned and abused, Jesus was dragged into an early-morning session of the Jewish ruling council, convened for this purpose (Mark

14:53). These leaders had coordinated the betrayal, dispatched the troops, and now awaited the trial. They'd already determined Jesus's guilt, so they needed only to extract an excuse that would justify a Roman execution (Matthew 26:59). The kangaroo court was now in session.

The council paraded many false witnesses to speak against Jesus. But they contradicted each other and couldn't get their stories straight (Mark 14:56–59). Even abetted by perjury, the religious rulers still didn't have any dirt on Jesus! For his part, like a Ranger POW, Jesus kept quiet and provided no useful intelligence to his enemies.

With their lines of questioning getting them nowhere, Jesus's accusers finally addressed the real reason he was there.

> The high priest asked him, "Are you the [Rescuer], the Son
> of the [heavenly Commander]?"
>
> Jesus said, "I AM. And you will see the [Rescuer] seated
> in the place of power at God's right hand and coming on the
> clouds of heaven."
>
> Then the high priest tore his clothing to show his horror
> and said, "Why do we need other witnesses? You have all
> heard his [false claims]. What is your verdict?"
>
> "Guilty!" they all cried. "He deserves to die!"
> (vv. 61–64)

Like a Ranger holding his position against an oncoming horde, Jesus never flinched as he confronted the death threats and verbal attacks of his enemies.

In their enthusiasm to see this presumed liar and false teacher dead, the religious leaders wasted no time acquiring a death sentence.

Although still early on Friday morning, around breakfast time, they made an unannounced house call to the Roman governor, Pilate. "They began to state their case: 'This man has been leading our people astray by telling them not to pay their taxes to the Roman government and by claiming he is the [God-promised Rescuer], a king'" (Luke 23:2).

Their first accusation was false. Just a few days earlier, they had tried to trap Jesus on the taxation issue, but he had evaded their snare, saying, "Give to Caesar what belongs to Caesar, and give to God what belongs to God" (Matthew 22:21). Besides, inciting tax evasion was probably not a capital crime. High treason, on the other hand, was.

> When you and I go into battle for God, we should not expect the other side to fight fair. ★

Pilate knew he had to look into this, even though he may not have wanted to.

So Pilate asked [the Rescuer], "Are you the king of the Jews?"
Jesus replied, "You have said it."
Pilate turned to the leading priests and to the crowd and said, "I find nothing wrong with this man! . . .
"Nothing this man has done calls for the death penalty. So I will have him flogged, and then I will release him."
(Luke 23:3–4, 15–16)

A mere beating would not satisfy the bloodthirsty religious rulers or the gawking crowd who had grown tired of this preacher from

Nazareth. Only a few days earlier, the same crowd had welcomed him into the capital as their long-awaited King. How quickly things had changed! Under pressure, Pilate reluctantly gave the execution order.

When you and I go into battle for God, we should not expect the other side to fight fair. Injustice is often the way of things. In the midst of it, we have to keep trusting and wait for God's ultimate justice to prevail.

Jesus's prejudiced trial and crowd-coerced sentencing was something like what a captured soldier might face in a foreign and hostile country. Would he be afforded a fair and unbiased hearing? Certainly not. In the same way, Jesus was treated as an enemy POW by a hostile government, though his own people perpetrated the injustice. Yet he remained silent and did not fight what he knew was a foregone conclusion. Like a Ranger, he accepted his fate with dignity and honor.

"Unjustly condemned, he was led away" (Isaiah 53:8).

THE TORTURE

At nearly noon, the Roman soldiers got ahold of their latest victim (John 19:14). It had been cold the night before, likely indicating a sky devoid of cloud cover (John 18:18). Now the sun was directly overhead. The Roman troops garrisoned in Jerusalem suited up in their battle rattle and no doubt baked in the Palestinian heat. As Jesus arrived, they took out their temperature-induced anger on this new target, attempting to have a little fun.

Jesus's first punishment was by the governor's troops. "[Pilate] ordered Jesus flogged with a lead-tipped whip" (Mark 15:15). They lacerated his torso and legs with a cat-o'-nine-tails thirty-nine times.[3]

The metal shards at the tips of nine leather straps would bruise and lacerate the victim's flesh when applied and rip holes in the tissue when removed. Rome often used this painful torture to deter crimes against the state. In Jesus's case, it served only to accelerate his death.

Jesus's next punishment was humiliation and more torture at the hands of Roman soldiers. The entire regiment came out for the show (Matthew 27:27).

> They stripped him and put a scarlet robe on him. They
> wove thorn branches into a crown and put it on his head,
> and they placed a reed stick in his right hand as a scepter.
> Then they knelt before him in mockery and taunted, "Hail!
> King of the Jews!" And they spit on him and grabbed the
> stick and struck him on the head with it. (vv. 28–30)

For some former POWs, the description of Jesus's torture is all too familiar. He was fatigued from the sleepless night, lightheaded from blood loss, dehydrated from heat, unbalanced from repeated blows to the head, and then stripped naked and spat upon.

While nothing can completely prepare a man for this type of systematic abuse, many special operations personnel complete SERE training (survival, evasion, resistance, and escape) to experience in advance what it is like to be captured and tortured. In SERE School, students are taught that no matter how painful the abuse and no matter what the indignities, they must not yield to their captors. They are never to give the enemy the satisfaction of breaking their will.

Like a SERE-trained Ranger, Jesus held firm to his mission. Defiantly, he clenched his jaw and said nothing. He endured the torment with his honor intact. When they finally tired of mocking him, they led him away to be crucified (Mark 15:20).

THE EXECUTION

Golgotha. It should be synonymous with the great battlefields of history. Antietam and Gettysburg. Ypres and the Somme. The sands of Iwo Jima and the beaches of Normandy. Because on that small hill just outside the city walls, a Hero gave his life to rescue humanity in the ultimate battle of history. Like a selfless Ranger, he willingly endured capture, torture, and death so that others might live.

After mocking and beating him, the four Roman soldiers on duty that day issued a cumbersome wooden cross kept at the city garrison for this purpose and ordered their victim to carry it (John 19:17). It was not a long walk from the judgment seat where Pilate gave the execution order to the hill where it would be carried out—less than half a mile.

A little after noon, the military detail arrived at the rocky knoll. Just as at his beating, Jesus was stripped naked again, his sweat-stained, blood-soaked garment taken as a gambling prize by one of his executioners (John 19:23–24). The soldiers likely laid the cross on the ground and threw Jesus down upon it, his shredded back grating against the roughly hewn timbers. Arms outstretched, his wrists were nailed to the crossbeam and his feet hammered into the post (Mark 15:24; Luke 24:39). With ropes, the detail raised Jesus to vertical until the cross dropped into the predug post hole, sending shockwaves of pain through its victim. The Warrior Christ—this divine Rescuer—hung helplessly to die, flanked on both sides by common criminals (Mark 15:27).

The mocking continued. The same mob who earlier that morning had demanded his execution gathered again to ensure that their demands were carried out.

The crowd watched and the leaders scoffed. "He saved others," they said, "let him save himself if he is really God's [Rescuer], the Chosen One." The soldiers mocked him, too, by offering him a drink of sour wine. They called out to him, "If you are the King of the Jews, save yourself!" (Luke 23:35–37)

Three years earlier, in the wilderness, Jesus had been tempted to use his divine powers to prove his identity and he didn't bite. Again, he showed Rangerlike restraint by not yielding to the taunts. Instead, he showed compassion for both executioners and mockers, praying, "Father, forgive them, for they don't know what they are doing" (v. 34).

> Summarizing his thirty-three-year mission on earth, Jesus said, "It is finished!" Using military vernacular, he would have said, "Mission accomplished!" ★

For several long hours in the heat of the day, Jesus endured the emotional abuse of the crowd as his body slowly succumbed to the cruel but effective Roman means of capital punishment. Never yielding, never showing weakness, he was the epitome of a SERE-trained warrior. Giving his captors no satisfaction, he faced death with calm strength and steely resolve.

What did the divine Rescuer think about during the hours when he hung on the cross? He had known for many years that this day was coming. This was the culmination of the Great Raid for which he was sent. The centuries of planning with his Commander and the years of preparing with his squad all led to this moment—the most critical aspect of any mission: actions on the objective. Only a week earlier, anticipating this event, Jesus told his disciples:

Now my soul is deeply troubled. Should I pray, "Father, save me from this hour"? *But this is the very reason I came!* (John 12:27)

He knew that he was right where he was supposed to be. He had to endure the painful ebbing away of his life on the cross.

Finally, summarizing his thirty-three-year mission on earth, Jesus said, "It is finished!" (John 19:30). In that short sentence (one word in Greek), Jesus effectively said, "Everything that the Commander asked of me has been perfectly executed and fully achieved." Using military vernacular, he would have said, "Mission accomplished!"

The final stanza of the Ranger Creed states, "Readily will I display the intestinal fortitude required to fight on to the Ranger objective and complete the mission, though I be the lone survivor." Jesus perfectly exemplified this ideal during his final hours. The mission required everything of him—he was emotionally abused, physically tortured, and spiritually sapped. Yet he never wavered from his objective. He fought all the way to Golgotha. Like many other soldiers in many other wars, he "took the hill" though it cost him his life. Flawlessly fulfilling his mission, he made one last radio transmission: "It is finished."

SERVANT TO PRISONERS

Like Jesus, his followers are called to be ready to give up everything in obedience to divine orders. For some, that "everything" is just as literal as it was for Jesus.

On the heels of World War II came the first Cold War conflict: Korea. Seasoned veterans took to war a new crop of young men, who were raised on stories of American military heroism. They expected the nation to support their cause, as they did for their fathers and older brothers. What they found instead was a war-weary nation that thought more about the Brooklyn Dodgers than the Inchon landing.

They were serving in "the forgotten war."

But a young priest from Kansas did not forget. Emil Kapaun could have sat out the conflict in his rural parish church, but he felt God's call to shepherd a different flock. Faithfully, he volunteered to deploy and minister to a new generation of warriors.

In November 1950, Chaplain Kapaun was ministering to his battalion as they fought in North Korea when he and many members of his unit were captured. Suddenly, this priest was a prisoner of war.

Many men in such circumstances begin to think of their own well-being, but not Father Kapaun. He worked tirelessly in the POW camp to care for his fellow prisoners. To improve their health, he dug latrines, smuggled in medicines, and even gave away his own rations. He also cared for their souls, providing prayer, counsel, and regular worship services, including an Easter sunrise service on March 25, 1951. Malnourished and suffering from dysentery and pneumonia, the beloved priest died two months later. Chaplain Kaupan was posthumously awarded the Medal of Honor for his actions both before and after capture.

Emil Kapaun ran through the finish line of life. He knew what awaited him on the other side, and so he willingly gave his life out of obedience to God and service to his men. How about us?

A CALL TO ARMS

The crucifixion proves just how physically and mentally tough Jesus really was. Can you picture the Sunday-school Jesus going through this torture? Can you imagine the meek Messiah up on the cross? His actions in his final hours show that he was bold, principled, and unafraid—far different than the docile weakling we sometimes make him out to be.

But more importantly, at the cross, Jesus demonstrated what it means to love. Now, I'm not talking about a Valentine's Day kind of love. There were no red roses or heart-shaped candy boxes at Golgotha that day. No, I'm talking about a Medal-of-Honor kind of love: putting your life on the line for your friends (John 15:13).

When I was at West Point, I had the privilege of hearing Ranger, author, and Vietnam veteran Stu Weber address a group of cadets. He told us three important lessons that the cross of Jesus teaches us about love—lessons that apply in every relationship, whether a soldier at war or a husband at home. I've never forgotten what he said, and I've shared it with many Rangers over the years. I want to share it with you too.

1. Love initiates.
Jesus didn't wait for us to cry out and beg for rescue. If he had, he'd still be waiting and we'd still be held captive. He also didn't wait for us to do something great enough to earn his rescue mission; he knew

we never could. Instead, he simply identified our need and came to save us. Love initiated the Great Raid.

The same is true for us. The warrior who dives on a live hand grenade doesn't wait for an order. Certainly, Marine Lance Corporal (and Medal of Honor recipient) Kyle Carpenter didn't have to be told what to do. He saw a threat that day in Helmand Province, Afghanistan, and smothered a grenade with his body. He identified the need and acted to save his fellow Marine. Now, that's love.

This principle works in the family too. Early in our marriage, I had a fight with Bree. I don't remember what it was about, but I remember that we weren't speaking. Even eye contact was off limits.

My wife and I were in the kitchen when God whispered to me, *"You need to do something to fix this."*

I protested, "But I'm not at fault! Why do I need to fix things?"

He simply answered, *"Love always goes first."*

A gentle touch on Bree's back melted our cold war.

Even today, you will have opportunities to live this principle. You can pick up the phone and call an estranged family member who may not deserve it. Or you can get up with a crying baby or a sick child when it's not your turn. You can fill up the gas tank or pick up some milk before being asked. Or you can empty the office trash or recycle bin just because it needs to be done.

Love doesn't wait for orders. And it doesn't ask if the person deserves it. It initiates. Love leads the way!

2. Love is costly.

"All gave some, some gave all." This phrase sums up the sacrifice that our veterans and our fallen have made.

Love always costs something. When Jesus came to earth, he knew that it would require everything from him. And yet he willingly demonstrated the greatest form of love: he gave his life for his friends.

Most of us will never be called upon to give our lives in battle as Jesus and Father Kapaun did. But we all can know the costliness of love. For me, I experience it the most with my three kids. My daughter will catch me with the last piece of berry pie à la mode and ask me for some. Love gives away. Or my boys ask me to turn off the game so that they can watch one of their shows. Love sacrifices. The more costly the act, the greater the expression of love.

> Love always requires something from you. ★

I'm sure that you, too, have experienced the costliness of love:
- Giving up a weekend to volunteer on a youth group retreat
- Staying late after work to help an associate complete a project
- Spending your savings on a costly anniversary gift
- Putting aside your plans to check in on a sick friend

Love always requires something from you. "For God loved the world so much that he *gave* . . ." (John 3:16). Love is costly indeed.

3. Love meets the needs of others.

Some people refer to the cross as a "demonstration" of God's love for us. It was so much more than that. When Jesus gave his life on Golgotha, he didn't merely show his love. He willingly went to the cross to rescue us from captivity and set us free. He met our deepest need.

When I'm teaching this concept to Rangers, I often use a silly example to prove the point. Imagine that I want to show my love to

Bree by going on a hunger strike. Yes, I initiated and it certainly will be costly, but how would that help her? She might instead ask me to fix dinners for a month or supervise the kids' bath and bedtime. You see, she doesn't really want a "demonstration"; she wants me to meet her needs.

As we seek to love those around us—our family, friends, and neighbors—we need to know and meet their needs. Cross the street and help a widow by cleaning out her gutters. Sit down with your ten-year-old and help him with long division. Offer to pick up the coworker whose car is in the shop. Donate or volunteer at a local food shelter so that the poor will have their basic necessities met.

Love is always focused on the needs of others. That is what Paul means when he says that love "does not demand its own way" (1 Corinthians 13:5). It seeks to serve.

You and I may never be in a situation where we must give up our lives in love for another. But in small ways we can initiate costly actions each day that will meet the needs of those around us. In that way we will be carrying on the mission of Jesus as we give our lives away.

———

The divine Rescuer was down. A Roman lance expertly thrust in his side confirmed it. Status: Killed in Action. But the story doesn't end there.

After Action Review

★ In Gethsemane, Jesus—the consummate Ranger
leader—focused on two things: his men and his
mission. What can we learn from Jesus's concern
that his men not fall into temptation? From his
concern that the Commander's will, and not his own,
would be done? How might this affect our prayers?

★ Jesus boldly confronted the armed guards who
arrested him. What does that say about his strength
of character? How do you think the Sunday-school
Jesus might have behaved? What does it say about
Jesus that he bartered his life to set his men free?

★ This book describes human beings as spiritual POWs
in need of rescue. How were Jesus's trial, torture,
and execution like what a POW might face? What
does it mean to you that Jesus volunteered for a
"prisoner exchange" on our behalf—our lives for his?

★ How is Golgotha (the hill where Jesus died) analo-
gous to a blood-soaked battlefield? How was Jesus's
behavior on the cross consistent with a mortally
wounded warrior? Does this metaphor show him
to be more like a Lion (Revelation 5:5) or a Lamb
(1 Peter 1:19)? Why?

★ What do you think of Stu Weber's three-part
definition of love? Why is it important that love
initiates? Is costly? Meets needs? Where do you
need to apply these principles in your life?

CHAPTER 10

Resurrection

The Honor of Looking Back on a Mission Accomplished

Surrender is not a Ranger word.

Look, the Lion of the tribe of Judah, the heir to David's throne, has won the victory. He is worthy [of honor].

— Revelation 5:5

In October 2003, after five months of combat in Iraq, I'd been promoted to captain and moved to the battalion staff. Lieutenant David Bernstein replaced me as the executive officer of Charlie Company. A West Point–trained Ranger graduate, David was an exceptional officer. I knew that I was leaving C Company in good hands.

In my new job as night battle captain at the battalion TOC (tactical operations center), I manned the radios on behalf of the commander. One night, listening to the reports coming in, I heard about an ambush that had just occurred. And I learned that David was involved.

In the initial barrage of gunfire, the driver of David's Humvee panicked and hit a berm alongside the road. The driver was ejected from the vehicle and pinned under the front left tire. The machine gunner, manning the pintle-mounted weapon behind the cab, was immediately killed by enemy fire. The vehicle was not armored, and David, sitting in the passenger seat, faced directly into the ambush line. An AK-47 bullet struck him near the groin.

Mortally wounded, David leaped from the vehicle and sought shelter on the leeward side. While other Humvees in the convoy deployed to destroy the enemy assailants, David jumped back inside, freed the trapped paratrooper, and continued to direct his men.

After the fight, David was evacuated. But it was too late.

Nearly two years later, I had the privilege of traveling to a small town in eastern Tennessee to help give his parents the honors their son had earned. In a ceremony with neighbors and friends, an Army colonel presented the Bernsteins with the Silver Star—the nation's third-highest award for valor—for David's selfless actions that night. As I listened to the colonel recount David's heroic deeds, I was proud to have served alongside such a remarkable man and to be there to honor one of our country's greatest warriors.

> Jesus sprinted through the finish line of his life, only to find glory and honor on the other side. ★

Any posthumous award ceremony is bittersweet. A warrior receives the honor due him or her, and we are challenged and inspired by the individual's heroism. Yet the soldier is gone and we are deeply saddened by the loss.

But in the case of the Warrior Christ, the story doesn't end with his death. His resurrection proves to each of us that there is life to be found beyond the grave. Jesus sprinted through the finish line of his life, only to find glory and honor on the other side.

Following his example, we, too, can run hard in this life—holding nothing in reserve—because we know what awaits us in the next. One day, either in this life or in the life to come, we will be able to look back with great satisfaction on what we have accomplished for God's kingdom and in his might. Whatever setbacks we may endure, the Enemy's final doom is sure. We are part of a victorious army!

Grief Turned to Joy

After Jesus's death on Friday afternoon, his Ranger squad spent the weekend hiding out in a house in Jerusalem. Contrary to their Leader's fearless example, these men were so afraid of suffering the same fate that they locked themselves inside (John 20:19, 26). Like a platoon of warriors who'd just lost their lieutenant, they sat together in silence, stunned by the outcome of their last patrol. As I imagine it, some shed tears. Others remained frozen. A few embraced one another, while others retreated to corners to be alone.

They simply couldn't believe that their Leader—the one whom they had believed was the Rescuer sent from God—had fallen in battle. Their sorrow over his death mingled with their guilt over abandoning him in his final hours. Any hope they'd had, the hope he'd given them, was now lost.

When several women left the house before dawn on Sunday to prepare the body for burial (forbidden on Saturday by religious laws), none of the men went along (Luke 24:1). After all, Roman guards were on watch at the tomb. Even now, with his body cold inside a hollowed rock, Jesus's opponents feared the postmortem impact of this revolutionary Teacher (Matthew 27:62–66). Going to the tomb would be too risky for his followers. Besides, who could bear to see their Leader reduced to a corpse? So the women bravely ventured out, while these timid men—belying their title as Rangers—mourned in hiding (Mark 16:10).

> The story of Jesus's resurrection isn't just about how he came back to life. It's also about a triumphant Hero who conquered his Enemy and lived to tell about it. ★

Not long after, the eleven-man squad was startled to hear the women shouting and pounding on the locked door. Why were they back so quickly?

The women breathlessly shouted, as if with one voice, "We just saw Jesus!" (see John 20:18).

"Impossible!" scoffed the men (see Mark 16:11).

Yet two Rangers decided to see for themselves. Peter and John raced for the tomb, and there they saw the same thing the women had: an empty shelf, with only some discarded wrappings where the body had been (John 20:3–8).

The story of Jesus's resurrection isn't just about how he came back to life. It's also about a triumphant Hero who conquered his

Enemy and lived to tell about it. It's about the battle scars that proclaim the Warrior Christ's victory. It's about the countless people
liberated by his selfless deeds, including you and me.

THE STORY TOLD IN BATTLE SCARS

As Peter and John returned, they too gave their testimony. Then, to
put all doubt to rest, Jesus showed up and spoke with the group,
showing them his battle scars.

> That Sunday evening the [Rangers] were meeting behind
> locked doors because they were afraid of the Jewish leaders.
> Suddenly, Jesus was standing there among them! "Peace be
> with you," he said. As he spoke, *he showed them the wounds
> in his hands and his side.* They were filled with joy when
> they saw the Lord! (John 20:19–20)

One Ranger wasn't there that night. Thomas missed Jesus's appearance, and when the other Rangers told him what they had seen,
Thomas probably thought they were pulling his leg.

Infantrymen are notorious for telling tall tales to their fellow
soldiers. I've heard all of the following over the years:

- "Go ask the supply sergeant for a box of grid squares."
  (Grid squares are found on a map.)
- "Find us a dozen chem light batteries." ("Chem lights" are
  chemically activated glow sticks. No batteries needed!)
- "Tell the first sergeant we need a bucket of prop wash,
  ASAP." (Prop wash is the current of air produced by an
  aircraft's propellers.)

- "Make sure you get the keys to the drop zone by 1400."
  (A drop zone is an open field where parachutists land
  during jumps. No keys required!)

Maybe Thomas, tired of being the butt of "Ranger games," decided he wasn't falling for this one. He demanded proof, saying, "I
won't believe it unless I see the nail wounds in his hands, put my
fingers into them, and place my hand into the wound in his side"
(v. 25).

Jesus back from the dead? Yeah, right! For more than a week,
Thomas resolutely held to his skepticism. Then everything changed.

Eight days later the [Rangers] were together again, and this
time Thomas was with them. The doors were locked; but
suddenly, as before, Jesus was standing among them. "Peace
be with you," he said. Then he said to Thomas, "*Put your
finger here, and look at my hands. Put your hand into the
wound in my side.* Don't be faithless any longer. Believe!"
(vv. 26–27)

Thomas's doubt crumbled when he saw the scars and touched
the wounds. The guys hadn't been messing with him after all. Their
Ranger Leader had made it off the objective . . . and was alive! Those
battle scars were primary evidence that the man standing before
them was the same man who had been crucified. Jesus's wounds told
the story of an epic battle.

Rangers love to tell stories. Ranger School stories. Deployment
stories. Stories of physical feats in the gym. But those wounded in
battle will do more than tell stories; they'll show you the scars. I have
heard many heroic tales and seen many horrific wounds.

- Staff Sergeant Oskar Zepeda suffered incredible damage to his right quadriceps and arm when an insurgent threw a hand grenade at his team as they were clearing a building. As I visited with Oskar in his office above the Ranger gym, he told me his story— what happened that night in northern Afghanistan and the many painful surgeries that followed. When I saw him one day in a PT (physical training) uniform, I could clearly see his massive wounds, especially on his leg. There was so much skin and muscle missing from his thigh that I could make out about six inches of femur behind the scar tissue. "You can touch it, sir," he said. "It doesn't hurt." Of course I did. His story was forever etched on his flesh.

- Sergeant First Class Ray Castillo lost both legs from an improvised explosive device during a dismounted raid near Mosul, Iraq. I have seen him put on his prosthetic legs and head to the gym for a tough workout, never complaining. He doesn't volunteer his story; real heroes never do. But if you ask, then he will tell you about that night, elevating the deeds of his men—especially the nineteen-year-old medic who saved his life—over his own. Ray doesn't need to flaunt his Purple Heart; his labored gait provides ample evidence of wounds received in combat.

- Master Sergeant Leroy Petry—the first thing you notice when you meet this humble American hero, after the broad smile filling his square jaw, is the mechanical hand peeking out from beneath his right sleeve. His story is well documented: Sergeant Petry received the Medal of Honor for picking up a live enemy hand grenade and throwing it away from his men, as it detonated. But if you saw Leroy in civilian clothes at a mall or with his son at the park, you wouldn't need to see a light-blue ribbon around his neck to identify him. His prosthetic hand—his ever-present reminder of battle—tells it all.

The scars on Jesus's hands, feet, and side also told a story. They provided graphic testimony of what he went through on a battlefield called Golgotha. Jesus neither hid his wounds in shame nor paraded them in arrogance—a Ranger never would. Instead, his scars served as a silent reminder that he actually did what he said he did.

"I was there," he might say. "I took the hill that day, as ordered by my Commander. Don't believe me? Here are the scars to prove it."

The Mission Effects

After a military operation, Rangers want to know about their effects on the target. They anxiously wait for confirmation. Did we get the guy we were after? Did we get his accomplices? Will the information we gathered keep them behind bars? They want to know that their efforts were not in vain, that they risked their lives for some purposeful gain.

We have described Jesus as the divine Rescuer, sent from God to save humanity. That was his mission. So, how well did he do? What were the after-mission effects of the Great Raid?

Scripture writers use two words to describe the impact that Jesus's thirty-three-year operation had on humanity: *ransom* and *redeem*. The words are closely related in origin and meaning but provide different metaphors for what the Rescuer has done for us.

Ransom secures release.

A ransom, by definition, is the instrument by which release or deliverance is made possible. A ransom satisfies the conditions for freedom.

> The scars on Jesus's hands, feet, and side provided graphic testimony of what he went through on a battlefield called Golgotha. Jesus neither hid his wounds in shame nor paraded them in arrogance — a Ranger never would. ★

In the 1996 movie titled *Ransom,* the son of a wealthy businessman is kidnapped and held for $2 million. At one point, the father, played by Mel Gibson, says, "I would pay ten times that if I thought it would bring Sean back."[1] In the 2009 movie *Taken,* the daughter of a former CIA agent is captured and sold as a sex slave for $1 million. Without hesitation, the father, played by Liam Neeson, offers to pay the broker that amount to buy her back, even though he has very little wealth. Both movies show loving dads who would go any distance, face any foe, and pay any price to win back their children.

As you can see, this is a perfect picture of the Great Raid. We saw earlier how, when Adam and Eve sinned, all humanity fell into a trap. Since then we have been held in a prison filled with toil, pain, sorrow, and death (Genesis 3:16–19). Yet all was not lost. As a loving Father, God was willing to do whatever it took to win us back. Though he owned all the riches in the world and would gladly have given every last treasure to rescue us, the demand price was not monetary. It was Jesus himself. Peter wrote: "For you know that God paid a ransom to save you from the empty life you inherited from your ancestors. And it was not paid with mere gold or silver. . . . It was the precious blood of [the Rescuer]" (1 Peter 1:18–19).

Jesus even spoke of himself as a ransom. Teaching his Rangers to follow his selfless example, he said: "Whoever wants to be a leader among you must be your servant, and whoever wants to be first among you must become your slave. For even the [Rescuer] came not to be served but to serve others and to give his life as a ransom for many" (Matthew 20:26–28). In other words, well before his death, Jesus understood that his life would be given as the means of release for many others.

Soldiers understand the concept of one life given in exchange for another. We recognize it when one of our own, such as Lieutenant David Bernstein, dies while rescuing his men. A half century ago, another paratrooper, an Airborne chaplain, did exactly that.

Chaplain (Major) Charles Watters was assigned to the 173rd Airborne Brigade in Vietnam. On November 19, 1967, during a devastating firefight, the company was forced to fall back and form into a perimeter to repel the enemy, leaving wounded paratroopers outside their lines. Repeatedly, Watters, a Catholic priest, rushed to their aid, grabbed the downed men, and hauled them back to safety, but he was mortally wounded in the process. Chaplain Watters was posthumously awarded the Medal of Honor for his heroic deeds. He lived Jesus's mission statement and gave his life as a ransom for many.

Redeem buys back.

The second word describing what the Warrior Christ achieved is *redeem*. It means "to purchase; to buy back" or, metaphorically, "to rescue from loss." The concept of being "redeemed" came straight from the slave market. Captured people were paraded on stage to be bought as slaves. Whoever paid the highest price "redeemed" the captive. One word Paul used to describe what Jesus did for us literally means "out of the market."[2]

> Jesus finished the mission concerned about only two things: fulfilling his Commander's intent and achieving the desired effects. ★

The slave market provides an excellent picture for the effects of the Great Raid. Spiritual slavery is a biblical idea. Jesus said, "I tell you the truth, everyone who sins is a slave of sin" (John 8:34). That's the bad news. But Jesus also introduced good news: freedom and adoption. In the next breath, he added, "A slave is not a permanent member of the family, but a son is a part of the family forever. So if the Son sets you free, you are truly free" (vv. 35–36).

Like a Ranger, Jesus finished the mission concerned about only two things: fulfilling his Commander's intent and achieving the desired effects. Offering his very life as ransom, Jesus paid the price to buy us out of the slave market so that we might be adopted into God's family (Galatians 4:5). I'd call that "mission accomplished"!

We need to hear this truth: we have a loving Father who willingly paid the ransom for our rescue. Many of my soldiers have never known a loving father. They come from broken homes, suffering either physical and verbal abuse or equally painful emotional neglect from their parents. Many of them joined the Army and chose the hardest possible assignment—the Airborne infantry—to prove their worth to worthless men who failed to be fathers. Perhaps you can relate.

Regardless of your dad's shortcomings, you have a Father who has not abandoned you with cold indifference but has pursued you with reckless abandon. You have a Rescuer who willingly paid the ransom price—his very life—to redeem you and bring you home. And the best part? He died to prove that you are worth it!

THE DECORATED HERO

As a nation, we love to celebrate the heroes of war. When they return home, these warriors don their dress uniforms so that a high-ranking officer can pin colorful ribbons on their chests. Purple Hearts. Silver Stars. Medals of Honor. Rife with significance, these small tokens express our country's undying gratitude.

Every year I look forward to our unit's Combat Awards Ceremony. A few months after we return home from deployment, the entire battalion—nearly one thousand Rangers—is on full display. Their jump boots shine, meticulously polished the night before, and their dress uniforms sparkle, silently telling the story of their service. As their chaplain, I get to look over this incredible formation of warriors from the podium before I bow my head and offer the invocation.

With friends, family, and a grateful public in attendance, Rangers to be honored are called forward. One by one, their names are read and their heroic deeds recounted. The ceremony concludes as all Rangers, past and present, stand to their feet and belt out the Ranger Creed in unison, pledging to "uphold the prestige, honor, and high esprit de corps" of the Ranger regiment. It gives me chills to hear my voice get lost in the roar, swallowed by the shouts of these brave men.

Jesus, a true Airborne Ranger, received similar honors when he returned home from the Great Raid. As the victorious Rescuer of humanity, Jesus received all the praises that his deeds deserved. While none of us is the Rescuer of humanity, one day our selfless actions in service of the King will also be rewarded. More on that later. For now, let's look at three honors Jesus received at his heavenly Combat Awards Ceremony.

1. His powerful location

In any kingdom or administration, the right hand of the highest ruler is the position of greatest honor. As the battle-scarred victor of human history, Jesus received this prized location.

> Now [the Rescuer] is exalted to *the place of highest honor in heaven,* at God's right hand. (Acts 2:33)

> Because of the joy awaiting him, [the Rescuer] endured the cross, disregarding its shame. Now he is seated in *the place of honor beside God's throne.* (Hebrews 12:2)

As part of his military honors, Jesus will forever sit beside God in the position of greatest esteem.

2. His mighty name

A man's name signifies his reputation. To honor his name is to honor who he is and what he did. Just as with great human warriors, names such as Pershing and Patton, we esteem the name of Jesus, remembering his heroic deeds in battle.

> God elevated him to the place of highest honor
> and gave him the name above all other names,
> that at the name of Jesus every knee should bow,
> in heaven and on earth and under the earth,
> and every tongue declare that Jesus Christ is Lord.
>   (Philippians 2:9–11)

> The [Rescuer] is far greater than the angels, just as the name
> God gave him is greater than their names. (Hebrews 1:4)

In chapter 2 I pointed out that Jesus's divinely chosen name means "the Lord is salvation" or "God rescues." For all eternity, whenever his name is mentioned, it will testify to his role as the divine Rescuer! "There is salvation in no one else! God has given no other name under heaven by which we must be saved" (Acts 4:12).

The name of Jesus is synonymous with his role. Like a cobbler named Shoemaker or a farrier named Smith, it is appropriate that Jesus will forever be called "God rescues," because that is exactly who he is and what he did.

3. His triumphant songs

Throughout Scripture, praise-filled songs are sung after great military victories (Exodus 15:21; 1 Samuel 18:7). These songs were meant to give honor and remember feats of bravery in battle.

Choruses about the Rescuer and his heroic deeds are repeated again and again by multitudes in heaven:

You are worthy. . . .
For you were slaughtered, and your blood has
        ransomed people for God
    from every tribe and language and people and
        nation. (Revelation 5:9)

Worthy is the [Rescuer] who was slaughtered—
    to receive power and riches
and wisdom and strength
    and honor and glory and blessing. (v. 12)

Blessing and honor and glory and power
    belong to the one sitting on the throne
    and to the [Rescuer] forever and ever. (v. 13)

The Warrior Christ received exalted honors following his actions in the Great Raid. For conspicuous gallantry in the face of the Enemy, he received a powerful position, a mighty name, and triumphant songs. Like a Medal of Honor, these decorations can never be revoked; they are his for all eternity.

> He fought on to the Ranger objective and completed the mission. Surrender was not in his vocabulary. ★

The resurrection turned Jesus from a fallen Warrior into a triumphant Hero. His wounds were evident, his effects hard earned, his honors well deserved. He conquered the Enemy, won our freedom, and lived to tell the story. He fought on to the Ranger objective and completed the mission. Surrender was not in his vocabulary.

We, too, are promised heavenly honors for a life well lived in service to God. Jesus promised that the "good and faithful servant" will be invited to "come and share [his] master's happiness" (Matthew 25:21, NIV). He further promised that those who are victorious in this life will join Jesus on his throne and will rule with him over the nations (Revelation 2:26; 3:21). But more than anything, these warriors will become children of the King (Revelation 21:7).

Now, that's a reward worth fighting for!

A Call to Arms

Rangers are taught to run hard through the finish line in any timed event. Whether participating in a five-mile run, a twelve-mile road march, or a four-hundred-meter sprint, no one wants the regret of looking at his time and wishing he had given more on the course. Rather, each man will fully expend himself, knowing that there is water, rest, or a meal beyond the goal. Similarly, Jesus sprinted to the cross and finished the race marked out for him, fully knowing there was resurrected life on the other side.

> We can run hard because we know what is beyond the finish line: rest for the weary and joy for a life well lived. ★

Jesus's resurrection proves that there is more vitality to be found on the other side of death (2 Corinthians 4:14). We would be wise to follow his example and run hard to the finish line of this life, trusting him for what's beyond our sight. When the Ranger Paul reached the end of life, he could say, "I have fought the good fight, I have finished the race, I have kept the faith" (2 Timothy 4:7, NIV).

How do we fight the good fight and finish well, as Jesus did? I believe that we can find three answers to this question in the opening verses of Hebrews 12.

- First, we "run with endurance the race God has set before us" (v. 1). I recently completed the Marine Corps Marathon, my first race at that distance. There were plenty of times that my body wanted to quit, but I knew that I had to finish what I set out to do. Life is not a sprint; you can't just go hard for a short season and then quit. There are no medals at the halfway point. You must finish the entire race. And in light of the resurrection of Jesus, we can run hard because we know what is beyond the finish line: rest for the weary (Matthew 11:29) and joy for a life well lived (Matthew 25:21).

- Second, we "fix our eyes on Jesus," who already started and completed his faith run (Hebrews 12:2, NIV).[3] When I am in the middle of a race, my mind sometimes wanders to the elite runners who are already finished. *They pushed themselves hard,* I think to myself, *and now their race is over.* When I imagine the finisher's medal they've already earned, I am motivated to earn one as well. Jesus also ran for a prize: "Because of the joy awaiting him, he endured the cross" (Hebrews 12:2). We can do the same thing in life. While athletes train for a temporary prize that fades, those who fix their eyes on Jesus are striving for an eternal reward (1 Corinthians 9:25). Focusing our attention on Jesus and the finisher's prize he has already earned gives us the motivation we need to run well and finish our own race.

- Finally, we remember the difficulties Jesus faced so that we "won't become weary and give up" (Hebrews 12:3). At the start of the marathon, I met a man who told me that most everyone hits a wall around mile twenty. Somehow, knowing that fact made it easier for me. When the trials came, I was mentally ready for them. If we follow Jesus into the fight, we, too, will face difficulties. In fact, Jesus promised them: "In this world you will have trouble." But he also gave us hope: "Take heart! I have overcome the world" (John 16:33, NIV). Everyone hits a wall in their spiritual race. The key is to remember the struggles of Jesus—and just keep running! The finish line is up ahead!

Jesus gave his life to rescue humanity—that's the story we were created to hear!

How do we find our purpose? We volunteer in his service—that's the mission we were designed to live!

———

The final picture is this: a defeated Enemy, a victorious Rescuer. The Warrior Christ's heroic actions proved him to be—in the fullest sense—the first and greatest Airborne Ranger.

After Action Review

★ Put yourself in the locked room that first Easter weekend. What is it like to lose your Ranger Leader, in whom you had such great hopes? What do you feel when the women or Peter and John return with news from the tomb? When Jesus himself appears?

★ Combat wounds always tell a story. What did the scars of Jesus say to his followers? Can you relate to Thomas's need for physical proof? What proof of the resurrection do we have today?

★ How was the life of Jesus like a ransom? How is God like the loving fathers in the two movies who would pay any price to rescue their children? What does this metaphor say about our situation before Christ's death?

★ The idea of God as Redeemer goes back to long before Jesus's time on earth (Job 19:25; Psalm 19:14). What does it mean to redeem something or someone? What does this metaphor say about our situation before Christ's death?

★ The resurrection proves there is life beyond death. Why should we "run hard through the finish line" in this life (see 1 Corinthians 9:24; Hebrews 12:1)? What does that look like for you? What are you holding back in reserve that you are unwilling to expend out on the course?

Taking Sides

Where Do You Stand?

While the battle may be over, the war rages on.

The highly decorated Warrior Christ never rested on his laurels. Since his death two thousand years ago, this hero has continued to take the fight to the Enemy, guiding his Ranger army—the church.

Admittedly, we don't always follow his orders. Sometimes we blow him off completely. Yet Jesus Christ never gives up on his mission or his followers. Despite our failings, he still stands at the front of the formation and faithfully "leads the way" for all who will follow.

> The LORD thunders
> > at the head of his army;
> his forces are beyond number,
> > and mighty are those who obey his command.
> > > (Joel 2:11, NIV)

BESIDE OUR LEADER IN WAR

As the consummate Ranger, the Warrior Christ stands shoulder to shoulder with us in battle, vowing, "I am with you always, even to the end of the age" (Matthew 28:20). He equips us for the fight, saying, "Put on every piece of God's armor so you will be able to resist the enemy" (Ephesians 6:13). He warns, "Stay alert! Watch out for your great enemy, the devil. He prowls around like a roaring lion, looking for someone to devour" (1 Peter 5:8). Our Leader knows firsthand the dangers of battle and wants his recruits to be ready for what we will face!

> I have commanded my holy ones;
>> I have summoned my warriors to carry out my
>> wrath. . . .
> The LORD Almighty is mustering an army for war.
>> (Isaiah 13:3–4, NIV)

But that's not all. The Warrior Christ has promised to come again and end this ancient conflict. And he won't come as a bureaucrat in a suit and tie to negotiate a peace treaty—that's not the Ranger way! He will come as both a battle-scarred Champion, skilled in warfare, and a conquering King, leading his army.

> I saw heaven opened, and a white horse was standing there.
> Its rider was named Faithful and True, for he judges fairly
> and wages a righteous war. His eyes were like flames of fire,
> and on his head were many crowns. . . . He wore a robe
> dipped in blood. . . . The armies of heaven, dressed in the
> finest of pure white linen, followed him on white horses.

From his mouth came a sharp sword to strike down the
nations. He will rule them with an iron rod. (Revelation
19:11–15)

This is no Sunday-school Jesus gently petting a fluffy white
lamb! This is Airborne Ranger Jesus coming with a sword to rid the
world of evil—once and for all!

Sound the trumpet in Jerusalem!
    Raise the alarm on my holy mountain!
Let everyone tremble in fear
    because the day of the LORD is upon us.
      (Joel 2:1)

BESIDE OUR LEADER IN PEACE

As excited as I am to take up arms with Jesus in this climactic battle,
I am even more eager for this war to end. I am ready for the day when
Christ the Conqueror achieves final victory and soldiers everywhere
hear his order to "stand down" forever. Ultimately, God will overcome evil and bring peace on earth. That means . . .

- no more flag-draped coffins or Purple Hearts,
- no more Gold Star families or widows dressed in black, and
- no more rifle volleys or names etched in stone.

All conflict will cease at last and we will finally have that long-
awaited peace. In that day:

The LORD will mediate between nations
    and will settle international disputes.

They will hammer their swords into plowshares
>   and their spears into pruning hooks.
Nation will no longer fight against nation,
>   nor train for war anymore. (Isaiah 2:4)

The boots of the warrior
>   and the uniforms bloodstained by war
will all be burned.
>   They will be fuel for the fire. (Isaiah 9:5)

Stoke the furnace! One day, warriors from every century of human conflict will incinerate their battle fatigues and combat uniforms. They will melt down their weapons to make something productive—no longer to kill and destroy, but to build and grow. All the training manuals and army regulations will become obsolete, kindling for the flames. War will be a thing of the past.

I can't wait!

> I am eager for the day when Christ the Conqueror achieves final victory and soldiers everywhere hear his order to "stand down" forever. All conflict will cease at last and we will finally have that long-awaited peace. ★

YOUR VITAL CHOICE

Will you join the Warrior Christ on his mission of ultimate liberty and peace? If you've made your decision, I invite you to take an oath of loyalty to this Ranger Leader by praying something like this:

I know that I am a slave to sin
and that you came to rescue me.
I want to follow you on your dangerous mission
and serve as your faithful Ranger, all the days of my life.
Amen.

If you just made that oath, then welcome to the Rangers! You have joined humanity's greatest Warrior as he accomplishes history's greatest mission. You are about to take up arms with him and charge the field against the Enemy of our souls. It won't be easy. The path ahead will be full of trouble, hardship, and danger—the typical Ranger triad. But here's a promise: fighting beside our Warrior-King, you will discover something in struggle that you never found in comfort—a full and meaningful life, a life of purpose.

If you've made that oath before, then you are already a warrior for Christ. You've signed up to follow Jesus in his worldwide Ranger mission—the Great Raid. Don't cower in a bunker. Don't hide in a fortress. God has made you for so much more! He has called you to "close with and destroy" the evil that plagues you, your family, and the world. This is the mission you were made for! What do you have to lose?

If you try to hang on to your life, you will lose it. But if you give up your life for my sake, you will save it. (Matthew 16:25)

Lock and load. It's time to join the fight.
Rangers Lead The Way!

Appendix

The Ranger Creed

Recognizing that I volunteered as a Ranger, fully knowing the hazards of my chosen profession, I will always endeavor to uphold the prestige, honor, and high esprit de corps of my Ranger Regiment.

Acknowledging the fact that a Ranger is a more elite soldier who arrives at the cutting edge of battle by land, sea, or air, I accept the fact that as a Ranger my country expects me to move further, faster, and fight harder than any other soldier.

Never shall I fail my comrades. I will always keep myself mentally alert, physically strong, and morally straight, and I will shoulder more than my fair share of the task, whatever it may be, one hundred percent and then some.

Gallantly will I show the world that I am a specially selected and well-trained soldier. My courtesy to superior officers, neatness of dress, and care of equipment shall set the example for others to follow.

Energetically will I meet the enemies of my country. I shall defeat them on the field of battle, for I am better trained and will fight with all my might. Surrender is not a Ranger word. I will never leave a fallen comrade to fall into the hands of the enemy and under no circumstances will I ever embarrass my country.

Readily will I display the intestinal fortitude required to fight on to the Ranger objective and complete the mission, though I be the lone survivor.

Rangers Lead The Way!

Acknowledgments

I must first give thanks and praise to the Lord Almighty, who called me to live and serve alongside these remarkable men, that I might know their hearts and speak their language. And, if that were not enough, then he gave me the passion and vision for this remarkable project. "Who am I, O LORD God, . . . that you have brought me this far?" (1 Chronicles 17:16). *Soli Deo gloria.*

I also want to thank my friend and mentor, Stu Weber, for his assistance throughout this endeavor. From the earliest manuscripts to the final product, your encouragement and support have proven invaluable. You are a true Ranger buddy!

And I must thank the remarkable team at WaterBrook Multnomah, who caught the vision for *Jesus Was an Airborne Ranger* and took a chance on an unknown author. In particular, I want to thank the editing team of Dave Kopp, Marcus Brotherton, and Eric Stanford. Your insights and inputs have both honed and strengthened the message of this book.

I want to thank the countless officers, NCOs, soldiers, and family members alongside whom I have had the privilege of serving during this nearly twenty-year journey. I especially want to thank the many chaplains who blessed me when I was an infantryman and who mentor me now as a chaplain. Your lives of service have found their way into my heart and onto these pages.

I must also thank my parents for the inestimable contributions they made to the man I have become. Mom, thanks for teaching me about the things of God and showing me how to lean on him in difficult circumstances. Dad, thanks for encouraging me to be a warrior, both in my personal and in my professional life. I am forever grateful for you both!

And last, I owe an inestimable debt of gratitude to my beautiful wife, Bree. Thank you for saying yes both to me and to this calling. Thank you for enduring the frequent moves and long separations that come with the military profession. Most of all, thank you for modeling for our kids what a wife of noble character looks like. "Many women do noble things, but you surpass them all" (Proverbs 31:29, NIV).

Notes

Introduction

1. C. S. Lewis, *Mere Christianity* (1952; repr., New York: HarperCollins, 2001), 46.
2. While the term *Christus victor* comes from Gustaf Aulén's 1931 book by the same title, it is based on the early church's ransom theory. For the first thousand years of church history, this view was supported by many great theologians, including Irenaeus, Origen, Athanasius, John Chrysostom, and Augustine.
3. *Badass* is defined as "a tough, aggressive, or uncooperative person." Jesus certainly met the first two aspects of the definition and, at least with respect to the religious leaders who tried to silence him, satisfied the third.

Chapter 1

1. The movie was based on two recommended books, *Ghost Soldiers* by Hampton Sides (New York: Anchor, 2002) and *The Great Raid on Cabanatuan* by William Breuer (Hoboken, NJ: Wiley, 1994).
2. In Scripture, Satan is called a deceiver (Genesis 3:13; Revelation 20:8) and "the father of lies" (John 8:44). His biggest lie is to convince us that he is good. As Paul states, "Satan disguises himself as an angel of light" (2 Corinthians 11:14).

Chapter 2

1. Shedding his abilities and becoming a human is, in fact, one subplot of the movie *Superman II* (1980), starring Christopher Reeves.
2. For more on Operation Husky, I recommend *Combat Jump* by Ed Ruggero (New York: HarperCollins, 2003).
3. Historians tell us that when Jesus was born, a sense of national pride was growing among Jews in Palestine, perhaps as a response to Greek influences or the ongoing Roman occupation. And so, many parents named their children after Jewish heroes of the Old Testament. Names like Mary, Joseph, Simon, Levi, Judas, James, and Saul all had ancient counterparts. Jesus too is the Hellenized version of the Hebrew name Joshua.

Chapter 4

1. For Gideon and Samson, see Judges 6:34; 13:25; and 15:14. For King Saul and King David, see 1 Samuel 10:6 and 16:13. For Ezekiel and Micah, see Ezekiel 11:5 and Micah 3:8.
2. Priests and priestly equipment were consecrated for worship this way (Exodus 28:41; 40:10–15). The first three kings of Israel were all anointed and set apart to lead God's people (1 Samuel 10:1; 16:13; 1 Kings 1:39).
3. Israel—specifically the southern Israelite kingdom of Judah— was under the control of the Babylonian Empire (586–538 BC), the Medo-Persian Empire (538–333 BC), the Greek Empire and the subsequent Ptolemaic Kingdom and Seleucid Empire (333–44 BC), and the Roman Empire (44 BC–AD 455).
4. Malachi, the last of the Old Testament prophets, wrote around 430 BC, or 460 years before Jesus began his ministry.
5. The story is brought to life in the 2002 film *We Were Soldiers,*

starring Mel Gibson. The movie was based on Lieutenant General Hal Moore's memoir, *We Were Soldiers Once . . . and Young* (New York: Random House, 1992).

6. This preferential choice of Christians to focus on only half of what Jesus did (either social justice or evangelism) is what World Vision president Richard Stearns has called *The Hole in Our Gospel* (Nashville: Thomas Nelson, 2009).

Chapter 5

1. Although the Scripture is silent on the relationship between the two men called "sons of Alphaeus," there is a strong chance that they were brothers. Early church father John Chrysostom said that both Matthew and James were tax collectors, putting them—at a minimum—in the same socio-economic level. In his book *Twelve Ordinary Men* (Nashville: Thomas Nelson, 2002), John MacArthur supports the potential of these two disciples being siblings, saying, "It could be that this James was the brother of Matthew. After all, Peter and Andrew were brothers and James and John were brothers. Why not these two?"

2. *Gladiator,* directed by Ridley Scott, DreamWorks SKG and Universal Pictures, 2000.

3. Martin Luther King Jr. said, "We must face the sad fact that at eleven o'clock on Sunday morning when we stand to sing 'In Christ There Is No East or West,' we stand in the most segregated hour of America." Fifty years later, his words still ring true. "Remaining Awake Through a Great Revolution," The Martin Luther King Jr. Research and Education Institute, http://mlk-kpp01.stanford.edu/index.php/kingpapers /article/remaining_awake_through_a_great_revolution/.

Chapter 6

1. *The Patriot,* directed by Roland Emmerich, Columbia Pictures, 2000.

2. You may choose not to drink for a variety of reasons. I absolutely respect that. My dad attended Alcoholics Anonymous for my entire childhood. We never had alcohol in the house—and for good reason! But please don't make the error of altering the historical Jesus to fit your convictions. As his followers, we must strive for an accurate picture of Jesus first and then live our lives based on that picture, not the other way around.

3. In World War II, American families displayed a blue star in the front window of their home or business, one for each family member serving in uniform. A gold star was then used to indicate a family member who had fallen in the service of the nation. The phrase "Gold Star" is used to describe those who have lost a Soldier, Sailor, Airman, or Marine.

Chapter 8

1. For more on the Ranger assault on Pointe du Hoc, I recommend *Dog Company* by Patrick O'Donnell (Boston: Da Capo Press, 2012).

2. I've cited Matthew's record of this teaching, which he places about a week earlier in Jesus's ministry. However, Luke's account of the same teaching occurs during this last meal (Luke 22:25–27).

Chapter 9

1. For more on the Battle of Mogadishu, I recommend *Black Hawk Down* by Mark Bowden (New York: Grove Press, 1999).

2. Some translations (e.g., NIV and NASB) put this statement of Jesus into a question, although that is not supported by the Greek verbs (both are imperatives or commands). Both the KJV and NLT (among other translations) use the direct statements, and given the context, I can't see any possible meaning other than sarcasm. (Of note, Mark 14:41 uses the same verb constructions.)

3. It was then believed that forty lashes would kill a man, so frequently thirty-nine were ordered (2 Corinthians 11:24).

Chapter 10

1. *Ransom,* directed by Ron Howard, Touchstone Pictures, 1996.

2. The Greek verb *ekagorazo* is found in both Galatians 3:13 and Galatians 4:5. It is composed of the prefix *ek* ("out of") and the root word *agora* ("market").

3. The Greek word *archegos* means "author," "founder," or "leader," and *teleiotes* means "perfecter," "completer," or "finisher." I think the writer of Hebrews still had the race metaphor in mind when he used these two words in 12:2.